An Anthropology of Services:

Toward a Practice Approach to
Designing Services

Synthesis Lectures on Human-Centered Informatics

Editor
John M. Carroll, *Penn State University*

Human-Centered Informatics (HCI) is the intersection of the cultural, the social, the cognitive, and the aesthetic with computing and information technology. It encompasses a huge range of issues, theories, technologies, designs, tools, environments, and human experiences in knowledge work, recreation and leisure activity, teaching and learning, and the potpourri of everyday life. The series publishes state-of-the-art syntheses, case studies, and tutorials in key areas. It shares the focus of leading international conferences in HCI.

User-Centered Agile Methods
Hugh Beyer
2010

Experience-Centered Design: Designers, Users, and Communities in Dialogue
Peter Wright and John McCarthy
2010

Experience Design: Technology for All the Right Reasons
Marc Hassenzahl
2010

Designing and Evaluating Usable Technology in Industrial Research: Three Case Studies
Clare-Marie Karat and John Karat
2010

Interacting with Information
Ann Blandford and Simon Attfield
2010

Designing for User Engagement: Aesthetic and Attractive User Interfaces
Alistair Sutcliffe
2009

Context-Aware Mobile Computing: Affordances of Space, Social Awareness, and Social Influence
Geri Gay
2009

Studies of Work and the Workplace in HCI: Concepts and Techniques
Graham Button and Wes Sharrock
2009

Semiotic Engineering Methods for Scientific Research in HCI
Clarisse Sieckenius de Souza and Carla Faria Leitão
2009

Common Ground in Electronically Mediated Conversation
Andrew Monk
2008

An Anthropology of Services: Toward a Practice Approach to Designing Services
Jeanette Blomberg and Chuck Darrah

ISBN: 978-3-031-01081-1 print
ISBN: 978-3-031-02209-8 ebook

DOI 10.1007/978-3-031-02209-8

A Publication in the Springer series
SYNTHESIS LECTURES ON HUMAN-CENTERED INFORMATICS #26
Series Editor: John M. Carrol, Penn State University

Series ISSN 1946-7680 Print   1946-7699 Electronic

An Anthropology of Services:

Toward a Practice Approach to Designing Services

Jeanette Blomberg
IBM Almaden Research Center

Chuck Darrah
San Jose State University

SYNTHESIS LECTURES ON HUMAN-CENTERED INFORMATICS #26

ABSTRACT

This book explores the possibility for an anthropology of services and outlines a practice approach to designing services. The reader is taken on a journey that Blomberg and Darrah have been on for the better part of a decade from their respective positions helping to establish a services research group within a large global enterprise and an applied anthropology master's program at a Silicon Valley university. They delve into the world of services to understand both how services are being conceptualized today and the possible benefits that might result from taking an anthropological view on services and their design. The authors argue that the anthropological gaze can be useful precisely because it combines attention to details of everyday life with consideration of the larger milieu in which those details make sense. Furthermore, it asks us to reflect upon and assess our own perspectives on that which we hope to understand and change.

Central to their exploration is the question of how to conceptualize and engage with the world of services given their heterogeneity, the increasing global importance of the service economy, and the possibilities introduced for an engaged scholarship on service design. While discourse on services and service design can imply something distinctively new, the authors point to parallels with what is known about how humans have engaged with each other and the material world over millennia. Establishing the ubiquity of services as a starting point, the authors go on to consider the limits of design when the boundaries and connections between what can be designed and what can only be performed are complex and deeply mediated. In this regard the authors outline a practice approach to designing that acknowledges that designing involves participating in a social context, that design and use occur in concert, that people populate a world that has been largely built by and with others, and that formal models of services are impoverished representations of human performance.

An Anthropology of Services draws attention to the conceptual and methodological messiness of service worlds while providing the reader with strategies for intervening in these worlds for human betterment as complex and challenging as that may be.

KEYWORDS

anthropology of services, practice approach, service design, service science, design and culture, design anthropology

Contents

Preface

We began to explore the possibilities for an anthropology of services a few years ago when two events in our lives converged. Blomberg took a job at IBM Research in a newly formed Services Research group after having spent most of her career in high tech companies developing approaches that integrated ethnography and design in the context of technology innovation. Around the same time Darrah was developing an applied anthropology master's program at San Jose State University and realized that graduates of the program would confront a world where services dominated economic activity and employment opportunities. We realized many of these newly minted applied anthropologists would find themselves among a growing number of workers who provide services to others or they would be hired to help companies, government agencies, and non-profits design services for their customers and constituents. Delving deeper into the world of services to understand both how services were being conceptualized today and the possible benefits that might result from taking an anthropological view on services became our focus.

This book in some ways reflects conversations we have had over the last few years both informally over coffee and more formally through a course we taught at San Jose State University on the Anthropology of Services and a paper session we organized at the first Human Side of Service Engineering conference, also on the Anthropology of Services. This Preface introduces the reader to the topics that have been the focus of our discussions and that led us to propose *An Anthropology of Services*. Central to our exploration has been the question of how to conceptualize and engage with the world of services given their heterogeneity, the increasing global importance of the service economy, and the possibilities introduced for an engaged scholarship on service design.

In effect, we invite the reader to share our journey. It is not one that arrives at a destination where the true or definitive view of services and their design is revealed; we claim no final answers or sublime insights that are ours alone. But we do claim that the anthropological gaze can be useful precisely because it combines attention to the details of everyday life with consideration of the larger milieu in which those details make sense. Perhaps most importantly, it asks us to constantly reflect upon and assess our own perspectives on that which we hope to understand and change. Our hope for an anthropology of services necessarily includes critique, but only as a prelude to action that is well informed and that ideally contributes to human betterment, as complex and vexing as that can be.

Our initial experience with services was from the start infused with our training as anthropologists. For us, this is where an anthropology of services begins, for we encountered an exciting and seemingly unexplored landscape of services which we unavoidably looked at with the professional naiveté of anyone trained in cultural anthropology. As we acclimated we found ourselves performing one of the oldest tricks of cultural anthropology: we saw the exotic in the familiar and the familiar in the exotic. Specifically, we could not help but frame familiar services and the language in which they were described as evidence of the exotic. It is this "exoticization" that helps provide anthropologists with the distance from social settings that allows them to ask different sorts of questions. From this perspective, getting a meal in a fast food restaurant, a ubiquitous and unremarkable activity for most Americans, is an extraordinarily complex set of performances by personnel and customers that have elements of both following scripts and improvising. It consists of actions that can be described, but it also depends on background knowledge that is often tacit, subtle interactions with built environments, and a keen sense of rhythm and coordination among strangers. It usually works as it should and when it does not, the participants typically are aware that something is amiss. Equally, we saw the familiar in the exotic when we encountered the ways scholars and practitioners were conceptualizing services. What was initially unfamiliar gradually came to be understood in many ways as parallel to what we knew about how humans have engaged with each other and the material world over millennia. For example, while the increasing reliance on fast food meals as a service can be seen as new and exotic, it can also be placed within a much larger cultural domain that is familiar to anthropologists. People, after all, eat together much of the time in all societies and fast food dining fits within a domain and connects fast food participants with one of the most familiar of human activities.

We initially entered the world of services because of its compelling interest to us as social scientists and because we recognized that it provided employment opportunities for our anthropology students and for ourselves. As we engaged people who were developing ways to understand and intervene in service worlds, we found that they made sense of our presence and interest in their work because of ethnography, a basic methodology of cultural anthropology. Although ethnography was relatively exotic a couple decades earlier, by now many people working in the field of services possessed at least passing familiarity with it. In some of the domains we were entering our presence was undoubtedly perplexing, but because service worlds were viewed as new and dynamic, it was not too far a stretch to see the potential of ethnography. After all, contemporary social life was now dominated by services, or so we were being told, and undoubtedly to understand it from the perspectives of those who were living it could be useful. Assimilating ethnography into a growing tool kit for service research and design seemed like a reasonable possibility.

However, our interests expanded far beyond that of conducting ethnographic research that would allow other professionals to do the work of designing services. We also were interested in contributing to the ways services were being conceptualized and in this regard we were fascinated by the ease with which researchers and practitioners could talk about services as clearly defined entities, out there in the world. When we looked around we saw a messier world of blurred boundaries, multiple perspectives, and divergent concerns. After all, services merged into—and drew upon—the rest of social life. Our conversations and interests shifted to a much broader anthropology of services and to a practice approach to designing services that included conceptualizing services and reflecting on the tools of service design as objects of study. We initially summarized our approach in a paper presented at the 2014 Service Design Conference (Sangiorgi et al., 2014) and subsequently revised as "Towards an Anthropology of Services" (Blomberg and Darrah, 2015). We have continued to elaborate and refine our thinking and the reader will find passages from our earlier publications integrated into the text of this book.

Our initial forays revealed the exotic and the familiar in the examinations of services, service worlds, and service design. We felt a great deal of humility as we encountered a landscape populated by people who seemed to know everything needed to make and remake service worlds. It was we who lacked the basic knowledge to effectively engage with these worlds, including even knowing the questions that made sense to ask. In this regard, like anthropologists more generally, we must have seemed at times confoundedly dumb or downright annoying with our initial "what's going on here and why" questions. But it is through questioning underlying assumptions that we begin to unpack the complexity of social life and discover new possibilities for acting.

Like many anthropologists we have long adopted a practice approach to our work. Darrah looked at workplace skills as they emerged from a community of practice (Darrah, 1997) and later at the practices of families managing busyness (Darrah, 2007). Blomberg studied the work practices of lawyers and civil engineers to inform the design of document management technologies (Blomberg et al., 1996, 1997; Suchman et al., 2002) and in her research on enterprise collaboration among service providers and their clients she applied a practice approach (Blomberg, 2008, 2011).

The hallmark of a practice approach is that it shifts focus from individuals who are often conceptualized in the design literature as "users" of services and products to a focus on practices themselves as the building blocks of society. By doing so, the approach explicitly draws the social into how we analyze everyday behavior and the contexts in which it unfolds. A practice approach also sensitizes us to reflect upon our own practices as scholars, researchers, designers, and organizational actors and how our practices shape what we learn and the actions we take.

In Chapter 1 we describe the anthropological lens through which we viewed services and service design. We outline key characteristics and foundational commitments of a practice approach and explore our motivations for taking a practice approach to designing services. We then review how our earlier research was guided by our background as anthropologists who adopt a practice approach. Finally, we describe where practices have helped us in our journey to understand the possibilities for an anthropology of services.

In Chapter 2 we describe the world of services as it was presented to us, with its transformative, world-making quality. We describe the growth in the service sector in developed and developing countries and discuss some of the drivers for this growth. We also note how services are being reconfigured by globalization and advances in technology, ushering in new models for how services are delivered including product-service systems, self-service, and peer-to-peer services. Finally, we begin to explore the implications all this is having on the labor force and on human-to-human interactions.

Chapter 3 begins to extend the anthropology of services by thinking of services as part of the human condition. We frame the discussion in this way very deliberately to draw attention to a rather shallow view of services in which they are treated as epiphenomenal to the rest of social life as compared to a deeper view in which they are at the core of being human. We ask the question of how people got on in the world before there was a service sector providing for their well-being. The answer rests, in part, on the observation that living in societies is how individuals have been able to survive and in this context people have always provided services to one another. By focusing on humans past and present we show how people have always created services or at least relationships and encounters that appear "service-like." Through an exploration of how services are integrated within societies, we argue that an anthropology of services can identify assumptions about familiar services and enlarge the scope for imagining new ones. In addition, we note that services and their effects are not limited to a service sector, but they come to define the connections people have to larger social worlds.

In Chapter 4 we take our anthropology of services in a different direction and focus our attention on the concepts that have commonly been used to conceptualize, analyze and design services. It is through these concepts that we initially engaged services and attempted to understand their relationship with anthropology. We look at how these concepts have been developed and assessed by people working within fields such as service marketing, engineering, information technology, and cognitive science. In this way we turn our anthropological gaze on those who have been in the business of conceptualizing and assessing services. We suggest that an anthropology of services will only be able to contribute to service worlds and service design through participation in communities of practice (Lave and Wenger, 1991) characterized by problem definitions, professional roles, analytical concepts, acceptable solutions, and methodological approaches. That said, we caution that communities of practice simultaneously limit options, arguing for the importance of reflecting on the taken for granted assumptions that underlie them. In the end our aspiration is to support a broader approach to understanding and intervening in service worlds.

In Chapter 5 we explore design particularly as it relates to service design. Most descriptions of design assume that humans have the ability to exert control and power over the world. However, there are complex linkages between ideas, the artifacts that emerge from those ideas, and the performances that bring ideas to life. Service design is not unique in needing to navigate and traverse the territory between idea and enactment, but for services the boundaries and connections between what can be designed and what can only be performed are complex and deeply mediated. In this context we consider the limits of intentionality, the meaning of unintended consequences, the boundaries between design and use, and inseparability of goods and services.

In Chapter 6 we turn to a discussion of recent developments in the field of service design, noting its rapid rise and close linkages to human centered design approaches. Our interest is in how services designers have understood the "objects" of design and the "acts" of designing. We describe some of the newer tools such as service blueprinting and customer journey maps that have been developed to support the design of services. Here we acknowledge the usefulness of such tools, while at the same time showing how they can distort and fail to recognize the multiplicity of relations that people have to the services they create and enact, and to the larger socioeconomic contexts in which the service exists.

In Chapter 7 we return to the point we have been making throughout the book that services are fundamentally social and we must understand this in order to create services that contribute to human betterment. In addition, we affirm the view that designers are participants in social contexts that shape their ability to engage with the service worlds they hope to effect. In this regard we outline a practice approach to designing that acknowledges that designing involves participating in a social context, that design and use occur in concert, that people populate a world that has been largely built by and with others, and that our formal models of services are impoverished representations of human performance. We argue that an anthropology of services, by providing a long view of services, can enlarge the scope of design while at the same time recognize the limits of design. An anthropology of services highlights the ways the relationships designers have to other people, both past and present, defines their ability to act and delimits the possibilities for bringing about something new.

Acknowledgments

This book began in conversations that started over a decade ago with colleagues in the Services Research group at IBM Research and found early expression in an applied anthropology course on services taught at San Jose State University in 2010—we thank those students for bearing with us. We especially thank three colleagues from IBM Almaden for their contributions to the journey described in this book. Jim Spohrer and Paul Maglio provided leadership and dedication in delineating a science of service. They and their writings stimulated and challenged us to articulate how anthropological ways of knowing connected to service systems and an emerging service science. Melissa Cefkin joined us in teaching the applied anthropology course and remained an ever-present interlocutor throughout our journey. She may see some of our conversations reflected in our writings although we bear responsibility for what has been put to paper. Steve Barley at Stanford University has long been a sounding board for our ideas and Diane Cerra at Morgan and Claypool demonstrated extraordinary patience throughout our journey. Finally our spouses, Richard Hughes and Janice Konevich, supported and encouraged us as we struggled to find the time needed to complete the book. Without them this book would not have seen the light of day.

CHAPTER 1

Getting Started

1.1 INTRODUCTION

This book is based on an intellectual journey we took as we explored the world of services and looked for meaningful ways to engage services both conceptually and practically. Before we begin to recount our journey, it is helpful to distinguish between what we took with us at the start of the trip from what we experienced along the way. Important for us is that we began and ended our journey as anthropologists who adopt a practice approach to understanding the human condition. We do not we claim that a practice approach is exclusively suited to exploring services, but from the start of our journey we expected it would allow us to see different facets of services than those most often discussed in the service literature and would provide insights to complement conventional approaches to service design.

Our decision to become anthropologists that we made long ago led us to explore some things and not others, and influenced where we ended up as we write this book. The discipline of anthropology is extremely diverse and so other anthropologists might follow different routes, but most would call into question or problematize the very categories used to understand the world. This requires a reflection on how we generate knowledge, what we think we know, and how methods of inquiry are simultaneously powerful and limiting. For example, when we set off on this journey we were predisposed to ask how the concept of service was being used to organize people's thinking about the world and with what consequences. We did not begin our journey looking for a single, correct definition of service, but instead we were interested in the consequences of how services are conceptualized on our ability to engage them in the world.

In this chapter we provide a kind of "bag check," opening our luggage to show what we packed before embarking on our journey and in so doing we introduce some of the basic concepts of a practice approach. The foundation of our approach to designing services lies not just in the books and articles we have read, but in what we have learned in conducting our research over many years as embodied activity whether for academic or practical purposes. Here we proceed by reviewing some of the research projects that have informed our thinking about a practice approach to designing services. Ultimately our interest is in the interweaving of practices and services, in the know-how that comes from journeying, and in how "service design" is enacted in the world.

1.2   PRACTICES AND APPROACHES

We need to distinguish the use of the word practice to refer to professions such as an architectural or medical *practice* from the day-to-day *practices* of architects or physicians. Our interest is primarily the latter: practices as they enable people to get things done in the world. It is inspired by social scientists such as Bourdieu (1977) and Giddens (1979), and usefully summarized by Ortner (1984, 2006). Subsequent theoreticians such as Reckwitz (2002) and Schatzki (1996, 2001, 2002) have built upon these foundations and we draw upon them here.

While there is no single, unified practice approach, most "...practice theorists conceive of practices as embodied, materially mediated arrays of human activity centrally organized around shared *practical* understanding" (Schatzki, 2001:2 italics added). This practical understanding is not simply knowing things about the world, but knowing how to engage in the world. "A practice is thus a routinized way in which bodies are moved, objects are handled, subjects are treated, things are described and the world is understood" (Reckwitz, 2002: 250). A practice approach views social order as emanating from the repetition of routines over time and is thus grounded in social reproduction. Change then occurs as everyday routines evolve in response to shifts occurring in social and material conditions and is sustained through knowing actors interpreting and responding to the situation at hand.

Knowledge is a critical element in a practice approach, but not primarily the propositional knowledge that individuals hold about the world. Instead, the focus is on the know-how required to get on in the world. This know-how is not located in individual minds, but is constituted through embodied practices where bodies mediate people's relation to the material world. This knowledge ultimately cannot be assessed by tests and quizzes, but by the enactment of practices—including the practice of test taking.

A practice approach draws attention to how practical knowledge arises and is replicated in the day-to-day activities of people. From this perspective, social life is composed of interwoven practices that are materially constituted. Schatzki reminds us that "this conception contrasts with accounts that privilege individuals, (inter)actions, language, signifying systems, the life world, institutions/roles, structure, or systems as defining the social (2001: 3)." From a practice perspective individuals are not the micro level building blocks of society, whether as minds or bodies. Instead specific practices consisting of activities, thoughts, and emotions; "things" used or encountered; and knowledge in the form know-how are the building blocks of social life (Reckwitz, 2002: 249).

To be sure, a practice approach does not replace existing vocabularies of social analysis, but it does reframe how they relate to each other. It blurs the distinction between body and mind, both of which are components of practices. Minds and mental phenomena are seen as embedded in activities of knowing and in the context of doing. Material things are not simply a backdrop to the practice, but they are integral elements, as indispensable as activities and knowledge. Reckwitz

(2002: 253) argues that "when particular 'things' are necessary elements of certain practices, then, contrary to a classical sociological argument, subject-subject relations cannot claim any priority over subject-object relations, as far as the production and reproductions of social order(liness) is concerned." Objects such as smart phones, offices, and even such mundane things as baked beans become sites of the social insofar as they are necessary components of practices. The social world thus is populated by practices carried out by actors who are neither completely autonomous nor handcuffed by norms: "They understand the world and themselves, and use know-how and motivational knowledge, according to the particular practice" (Reckwitz, 2002: 256).

By adopting a broad, overarching practice approach we acknowledge that a variety of insights and perspectives have informed our and others' understanding of practices as constitutive of social life. We suggest that ethnomethodology (Garfinkel, 1967; Heritage, 1984; Lynch, 2001) and actor-network theory (Latour, 1987; Law, 1992, 2009) have a deep affinity with our practice approach in for example the way ethnomethodology directs our attention to how order is practically achieved in and through human action and the way actor-network theory focuses attention on the role of materiality and non-human agency in configuring the social. A practice approach we contend welcomes these perspectives while not insisting on a strict adherence to them.

As we have noted, our exploration of a practice approach to designing services is grounded in our backgrounds in anthropology and we also draw upon some of anthropology's basic tenets to guide us. As anthropologists we focus on how people act in particular situations, and how their actions are understood within larger social milieus. We pay close attention to different perspectives, being careful to note the distinction between insider and outsider views. Capturing the perspectives of insiders drives us toward careful description that distinguishes among the things that make sense to the people we study. In adopting this stance, sometimes referred to as an emic perspective, we do not ask if people are right or wrong, but how do they understand and act in the world around them and see their place within it.

As anthropologists we also recognize that an outsider perspective on understanding the human condition, sometimes referred to as an etic approach, is necessarily a feature of any community of scholars or expert practitioners who draw distinctions to help them understand and act in the world they gaze upon. Disciplines or fields of study are characterized by approaches where expert practitioners learn to apply a set of concepts to help them systematize knowledge and thereby promulgate particular understandings of the world. Although expert practitioners sometimes accept "their" perspectives as natural and obvious ways to see the world, these perspectives too reflect their interests and assumptions and as such they can be studied for the insider perspective they reveal. Anthropologists are keen to consider their own taken for granted assumptions, questioning the very categories they use to understand the world.

As anthropologists we ask how people make themselves and the social world they live in through their actions and those of others. Answering this question requires looking in detail at people's everyday practices and how when taken together they constitute social life. But what does it mean to focus on people's everyday practices; how might we go about doing so; what insights about the human condition might follow from looking at the world through a practice lens? Like all theoretical approaches, a practice approach provides a set of concepts for looking at the world and it guides us to see some things and not others, and to analyze what we see in particular ways. Broadly speaking our practice approach to designing service reflects our backgrounds as anthropologists interested in a social science capable of generating useful knowledge with practical implications.

1.3   OUR PRACTICES AS ETHNOGRAPHERS

Over the years we have adopted a practice approach to help us understand particular social settings, from workplaces to families. Darrah (1992, 1997) conducted fieldwork on the shop floors of a manufacturer of specialized wire and cable products and of an assembler of computer work stations marketed to several professions. Later, he and two colleagues looked at how people juggled and balanced the commitments of work and family through fieldwork with dual-career families (Darrah, 2006; Darrah et al., 1997; 2007). Blomberg and her colleagues studied the practices of lawyers and document coders working at a Silicon Valley law firm and engaged these workers in the design of document management technologies (Blomberg et al., 1996, 1997). They later expanded the focus to include the document practices of engineers designing a bridge (Suchman, 2000). Blomberg subsequently explored enterprise collaboration within firms providing IT services and between those firms and the clients they served (Blomberg, 2008; 2011; Cefkin et al., 2007).

A practice approach has been salient for us in two ways. First, our practices as ethnographers are salient as they shift attention away from viewing research as a set of logically necessary steps toward seeing research more as a concatenation of activities that ultimately result in knowledge claims—what others have referred to as a kind of bricolage (Levi-Strauss, 1966). Our fieldwork can thus be understood using concepts provided by a practice approach and doing so allows us to better understand the knowledge claims we make. We also conduct fieldwork in order to learn about practices in the world that are salient to addressing concerns in families, communities, organizations, and most broadly in society. Ethnographic fieldwork is sometimes portrayed as almost journalistic in its capacity to recount the experiences of people, but our intention has always been to use the intimacy it rests upon to identify practices that have wider currency. In this way, what seems personal and even idiosyncratic is linked to the very foundations of social life—how people get things done in the world.

Because we entered workplaces and the lives of families as ethnographers taking a practice perspective, our research took specific form. It required being present in the social settings in which we found ourselves and knowing how to fit into them as participants while still maintaining enough distance to record and reflect on what we saw, heard, and experienced. By "being there," whether physically or virtually, we were able to directly engage with people and learn about aspects of their world that they otherwise might find difficult to tell us about in the abstract.

Being there also enabled us to build trust, something that cannot be requested but must be earned. We found that often the relationships between where trust was earned and where it was ultimately salient were complex and indirect. The trust established by being there also allowed for reciprocal interactions and exchanges that were critical for keeping our projects moving forward. Being there allowed us to engage people as partners with whom we could identify and explore areas of mutual interest, recognizing that they were to us far more than research subjects. Darrah, for example, would get phone calls at home or would be approached at the field site by people who would say, "You know I was thinking about…" clearly demonstrating that they were engaged in the project and pushing it beyond the researcher's presuppositions. Blomberg and her colleagues directly involved study participants in thinking about how possible changes in the material conditions of their work brought about by the introduction of new technologies and organizational processes might transform their work lives. From their varied perspectives participants in their projects became invested in the outcomes of their collective efforts.

Many of the families described in *Busier Than Ever!* (Darrah et al., 2007) participated in the study precisely because they believed this would give them a chance to explore and reflect on their lives, and even assess "how are we doing." This led Darrah to look at family life as an ongoing stream of everyday experiments where families moved between replication and variation of routines. While the notion of routine might suggest bland predictability, the lives of these families were characterized by a creative tension between experimentation and business as usual. This meant that Darrah too needed to remain open and not create a comfortable, but artificial or misleading, sense of closure and finality.

Similarly, participants in Blomberg's law firm study saw the project as an opportunity to reflect on their own practices and how new technologies might significantly change their day-to-day work lives. That said Blomberg and her colleagues became keenly aware that the law firm participants had been tinkering with their work lives long before the researchers arrived on the scene and would continue to do so after they left. But as they engaged with prototypes introduced by the researchers, the participants acquired an embodied understanding of what it would take to integrate new document management technologies into their routines, allowing them to assess whether and under what conditions it would make sense to do so.

Because we were able to stay engaged in our field sites for a long enough period of time to experience shifts, and in some cases to provoke them ourselves, we were able to see both the replication of routines and the often subtle changes in those routines. Fieldwork in this sense is more like a movie with a plot that unfolds through time than a series of snapshots mounted in a scrapbook. It is the movement from scene to scene, the unfolding of activities, where practices are enacted. Part of our know-how as ethnographers then was in managing relations with participants so they continued to be interested in what might come next. They came to understand our interests and we learned what they cared about. In the process narratives emerged that reflected what mattered to people in different ways.

Ethnographic know-how also meant being able to negotiate intimacy and distance. Darrah, for example, was assimilated into the families he studied in part because they were already familiar with notions of pseudo-kin and family friends that allow outsiders to participate in the lives of families. Indeed Darrah's social distance mattered—it was what made it plausible for him to be present at all given he was not a member of these families. If not well managed then someone might conclude "you're not one of us so why don't you just leave and make our lives simpler?" Over time, being trustworthy and interesting to these families was prized and the families gradually incorporated the ethnographer into their lives. This allowed Darrah such opportunities as being an audience for family arguments, attending PTA meetings, and helping to shop for gifts for the children since it was assumed he knew best their preferences from the extensive time he spent talking with them.

A different bundle of issues emerges when studying workplaces where participation by workers is sometimes constrained. Darrah shadowed a fireman for days at a time, but did not pitch in when something was aflame. In general, he hung out in the spirit of participant observation and participants would explain what they were doing and why, and overtime his questions became more refined. Eventually, explanations were offered without probing and eventually the ethnographer becomes adept at a sort of anticipatory internal accounting for action. For example, after months of observing on the shop floor, Darrah would imagine what a machine operator was looking at and for, and anticipate their next move—he was in a sense operating machines in his mind. If there were gaps between his expectations and what machine operators did then he would ask and they would respond quite naturally. All this entailed imagining and then asking about the gaps in sequences of activities. In effect, Darrah as the ethnographer, created both description *and* the missing elements when he proposed a strings of activities. And throughout his tone and body language mattered as did expressions of interest that came from participating in the moment, if only as an observer.

In Blomberg's project exploring the practices of civil engineers designing a bridge (Suchman, 2000), she prompted one of the engineers to file project documents that had piled up on drafting tables. While she sat and observed, she took the opportunity to ask for clarifications and to see if her understandings of the "requirements" of the work fit the situation at hand. This was done to give her a chance to see firsthand the practices of filing project documents, an activity that only occurred every now and then. In Blomberg's research on enterprise collaboration occasionally she found herself the "observer" of conference calls, a frequent component of the work of employees of large multinational firms. This involved not only listening in on the calls, but also reviewing the documents distributed to participants before the calls, and later following up with participants to fill in missed details and to get their take on what had transpired during the calls. In some instances she also was present in the conference room where people had assembled to take the call together.

This gave Blomberg the opportunity to observe the interactions going on in the room that were not visible to remote participants. Fieldwork always requires a level of creativity in finding the right opportunities to be present for the everyday flow of events and activities. This is both a practical matter and a theoretical one, and it reflects the shifting interplay of participation and observation.

As we noted, the material world is neither mere backdrop nor does it in any simple way have independent, salient characteristics that determine action. The material characteristics of a setting become implicated in practices and at the same time practices give the materiality of the setting saliency in specific ways. For example, the wire and cable factory Darrah studied was a cavernous gloomy interior containing machines with properties that came into play when they were used in specific ways. There was a dance between things and people, the choreography of which the ethnographer needed to describe. These material conditions did not simply and directly drive routines, but they configured the possibilities for action. For example, managing or dampening the effects of variances in machine performance, inputs, or environmental conditions was key to being a skilled practitioner. But an operator's practices also created variances, making them salient in particular situations. Newer digitally controlled machines changed the variances and in some cases eliminated or altered long-standing practices, as when plucking wires to assess tension was assimilated by a computer function that eliminated tactile skills and added abstract digital ones.

Even when the work primarily involves the processing of information such as in the work of designing IT infrastructures that Blomberg studied, the material conditions help define what is possible and how activities unfold. For example, spreadsheets represented years of organizational knowledge about the costs of managing various alternative IT infrastructure designs. It was through the practices of the "solutioners," as these designers were called, that this organizational knowledge was made available and passed down over the years. The exact origin of the spreadsheet templates was not known to the solutioners, but these tools of the trade continued to be essential components of their work practices.

Families, too, presented contrasting ways of creating and engaging material conditions. The Carlsbergs, one of the families in Darrah's study, embraced Pokémon cards that simultaneously demonstrated parental commitment ("this is what you do for your kids—get up early to get the latest shipment"), the value of a particular lifestyle and artifacts, and the arithmetic skills needed to calculate card values as a basis for school success and ultimately building a professional career.

Ethnographers observe, probe, and reflect on what they see. Take, for example, two people playing with a child. This can be seen as parents enjoying "family time" or alternatively as childcare services being provided by workers at a daycare. The distinction may not be obvious at first, but the practices appropriate to each will differ. Assessments of proper care, down to touching, depend on knowledge of the extant relationships and significance of the activities. Further layers of ambiguity can be introduced if the relationships between childcare providers and parents persist. Darrah, for example, studied a couple who had a long-term relationship with a husband and wife who provided care to their two children. The arrangement brought together a pair of politically liberal Democrat parents with a pair of conservative-minded Republican caregivers. Despite the dramatic differences in political views and values, the parents acknowledged that elements of the caregivers' values had become "our family values" and that the relationship was more than one between service provider and recipient, regardless of how it began. These two couples initially came together for their own purposes and then discovered that they had become entangled in unexpected ways that challenged clear and familiar boundaries, transactions across them, and interactions among them. Although not all relationships between service providers and recipients become as complex and long-standing as this one, the story reminds us that services are often more nuanced and ambiguous than is sometimes suggested by their descriptions in the literature. Services always are embedded in and unfold within situation-specific contexts that give them their meaning.

Ethnographic fieldwork privileges localized actions and structures (practices), which can constrain our understandings if we conclude that what we have been able to witness and be part of tells the whole story. Activities, people, and events far removed from local settings are salient to what is occurring locally. Yet accounting for these distant factors can be tricky and it can tempt researchers and practitioners alike to propose that larger "systems" are responsible for what occurs locally. But these distant conditions are also very specific and viewing them as part of systems can do more to obfuscate than reveal the relations among things local and distant.

1.4   BON VOYAGE

Our journey into the world of services and their design draws upon these lessons we have learned from our training as anthropologists and the myriad of projects we have been involved in over the years. Just as participation in the local scene was essential for our understanding of these various sites, so it was for our journey into the world of services. We did not proceed just by asking experts or reviewing literatures, but by engaging services and service design ourselves as researchers and practitioners.

For us it has been important to problematize the basic concepts and activities we encountered on our journey. Simple assumptions had to be challenged and boundaries pushed by questioning, for example, the saliency of such measures of services as cost, productivity, and efficiency. We also found it useful to situate services in a temporal dimension and ask in what ways services were new as we reflected on the ways services were both the same and different throughout time. And all along we looked for the material embodiments of services as enacted and as evidenced by the know-how of participants.

As we prepared to depart we were reminded of the admonition familiar to generations of ethnographers—to keep an open mind. Yet as we began there were several distinctions that we knew would guide our journey and, ultimately, this book. We summarize these distinctions with a simple diagram that sensitizes us to look for practices in a number of places and to understand how they intersect with services. Throughout the chapters of this book we will focus on each in turn.

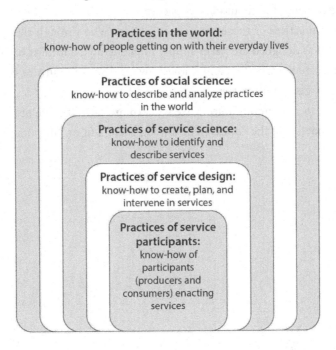

Figure 1.1: Practices.

Most broadly are the practices of people getting on with activities in their everyday lives. These practices include those of aboriginal hunting bands, terrace rice farmers, and early Industrial Revolution loom operators, as well as the practices of contemporary societies. From this perspective practices are ubiquitous in the human record, and the discipline of anthropology takes pride in documenting them.

Second, are the practices of social scientists and other professionals whose know-how is used to discover, describe, and analyze practices in the world. These professionals in effect learn how to "see" practices in the world from what people say and do.

Next, are the practices of service scientists who describe services using concepts that are intended to be universally applicable. They define a language of services where concepts like service encounters and service systems are used to characterize services and it allows them to explicate and identify services from among all the ways humans engage the world around them.

Fourth, are the practices of service designers and other professionals who seek to create services and in so doing bring about change. Using the language of service scientists and through abstract representations of services they aim to intervene in the world. Their abstract representations of services—i.e., blueprints and customer journey maps—become tools for deciding how things might be different and for accounting for how participants will enact the service as it moves from drawing board to the realm of flesh and blood people.

Finally, are the practices of those who enact services, who through their know-how engage with services. Services as designed are never simply implemented, but must be actively taken up by people with particular motives, bodies, and know-how. And so we return to where we began with the practices of people getting on in the world.

As we continue to recount our journey we will explore each of these practices and the know-how they imply to understand the connections among them and to inform a practice approach to designing services.

CHAPTER 2

From Services to Service Worlds

When we first encountered the literature on services we were struck by the transformative character of the discourse. We were being reminded that modern economies had become service economies and in time services would dominate the economies of the rest of the world. While this discourse seemed a bit hyperbolic, it pointed to a change akin to the transition from agriculture to manufacturing, with all the attendant adjustments and adaptations. We had to ask ourselves if we were in the middle of another major shift in how people got on in the world. And, if so, how was the world we inhabited being reconfigured and what ability might we have to shape it through intentional acts of design? As anthropologists it seemed we could ill-afford to ignore changes marked by a major shift in economic activity, after all anthropology had long examined how differences in "the means of production" were associated with particular sociomaterial arrangements (Johnson and Earle, 1987; Plattner, 1989).

The literature on services stressed how service economies were less focused on the production of material things, a characteristic of industrial societies, and more focused on the transformation of state, for example, from dirty to clean (cleaning services), from ignorant to informed (educational services), or from sick to healthy (healthcare services). Services were being distinguished from goods with most definitions including some mention of the intangibility of services and their inability to be possessed, stored, or transported (George and Berry, 1981; Lovelock, 1996; Zeithaml and Bitner, 1996). Services, it was argued, only existed at the time of their consumption, when skill and expertise are applied to achieve a transformation or produce some outcome. The literature also noted how services were co-produced through interactions between providers of the service and those who "consumed" or received the service. And equally important, the value of the service was dependent on particular relationships between service providers and consumers. We wondered in what ways an economy increasingly fueled by services with these characteristics was changing the sociomaterial conditions in which we lived. How were these purported differences between products and services having an impact on the practices, the day-to-day activities of the growing number of people involved in services as their producers, consumers, and designers? It seemed that services were possibly world-making in that their success required people who recognized and valued the transformations brought about by a changing and expanding collection of services.

2.1   CONTEMPORARY SERVICES

As we began to look more closely at contemporary services, we asked some basic questions. What activities were designated as services and why? How was the world being affected by the growth of the service economy worldwide? What was fueling this growth? What impact was this growth having on employment and the kinds of jobs available to people? And throughout this exploration we reflected on what the perspectives of anthropology and a practice approach might teach us about contemporary services.

2.1.1   DIVERSITY OF SERVICES

One of the first things we were stuck by was the sheer diversity of services. They included the hands-on services of janitors, teachers, doctors, and chefs; the technology-mediated services of automated bank teller machines, self-service checkout lanes in grocery stores, and online travel reservations; and the business-to-business services of IT outsourcing, package delivery, and insurance claims processing. Services also differed markedly in complexity. For example, the services of a massage therapist are relatively simple and direct where those of an accounting firm providing financial and legal services can be very complex, including that they sometimes are delivered indirectly by people or firms geographically dispersed. Services also differ in terms of the skill and education required to both deliver and consume them. For example, many healthcare services require extensive training and credentialing to perform, whereas the fast food servers may need little formal education with training taking only hours or days. Moreover, recipients of services also differ in what is required of them to be able to consume services beyond simply the financial where-with-all to pay for them. For example, mom-and-pop businesses may not have the technical infrastructure or know-how to utilize the services of cloud computing firms. Likewise, self-service offerings such as grocery self-serve checkout or online travel reservations may be less available to people who lack familiarity with computers and their interfaces.

This diversity of services has meant that services are viewed from many different perspectives by both researchers and service providers. For example, engineers often focus on how services are mediated and enabled by IT (Karwowski and Salvendy, 2010), whereas marketing professionals are more concerned with the economic value of services (Teboul, 2006), and citizen activists and policy makers are attentive to the equity and fairness of services (Åkesson et al., 2008), including those delivered by government agencies. The particular perspective taken to understand services and service worlds undoubtedly influences our ability to manage their impact and shape their design.

2.1.2 SCALE OF SERVICES

In our exploration of services, almost everywhere we turned we were hearing that services are trans-forming economies on a scale reminiscent of the earlier transition from agriculture to the industrial age. Not only was there a diversity in what is designated as a service, but when taken together the scale of services was sizable and growing, both in terms of number of jobs and GDP. For example, over the last seven decades in the United States services as a share of total GDP rose from 60% to 80%. This growth is mainly attributable to a growth in three sectors: professional and business ser-vices, finance and real estate services, and healthcare services. The employment increases associated with this growth in GDP has been substantial but uneven, with professional and business services experiencing the largest growth while employment growth for finance and real estate services lag-ging behind the rise in their contribution to GDP (Berlingieri, 2013). Similarly, among the OECD economies the service sector now accounts for over 70% of total employment and is responsible for almost all recent employment growth (OECD, 2005). Between 2000 and 2013 employment in the service sector grew by over 5% worldwide with a rise to 74% in the so-called developed economies and 45% of worldwide employment (Global Employment Trends, 2014:96).

2.1.3 DRIVERS OF SERVICE GROWTH

Bryson et al. (2004) identify some of the drivers of the growth in services in the developed coun-tries. First, as per capita incomes have increased so has the demand for services. Among high paid segments of the population there is a growing reluctance to use scarce non-work hours for chores and repairs. Instead, people are choosing to convert non-work hours into a demand for services. This drives both an increase in service production and consumption, as well as in the variety of both consumer and business services. In addition, there is an increasing demand for healthcare services in part brought about by changes in population demographics, the rise in chronic diseases such as diabetes, an emphasis on wellness and preventive medicine, and the availability of new treatment modalities. Likewise, there is an upswing in demand for educational services as changing labor markets and the increasing requirement for skilled workers result in the need for a more educated populace. Finally, the increasing size and role of the public sector generates new policies and reg-ulations that must be navigated, often with the help of professionals such as social workers, tax advisors, and attorneys, adding to the growth in service employment.

Other drivers of the growth in the service sector are globalization and technological ad-vances. Many services can now be sourced from abroad as an alternative to in-house production of services. Companies engage firms that specialize in providing services needed to run their busi-nesses including such services as human resources, finance, IT, and customer relations management. In addition, the development of broadband networks and the digitization of services, along with changes in regulatory policies, allow work to be done beyond country borders by an increasingly skilled international labor pool. There are many reasons why businesses decide to outsource some of their internal functions, including to increase their focus on the core elements of their business, mitigate against risks of a volatile economic climate, secure expertise they do not have or wish to acquire, and establish strategic alliances with other companies. As organizations divest themselves of functions and externalize or outsource them, new boundary-spanning services are created to manage and coordinate activities between organizational entities.

2.1.4   SERVICE GROWTH IN DEVELOPING COUNTRIES

While the size of the service sector as a percentage of GDP is smaller in developing countries the growth in services has been identified as a strong contributor to poverty reduction in developing countries. The linkage to poverty reduction is strengthened by the fact that the proportion of women employed in services is often higher than for manufacturing and their employment opportunities are closely associated with rising incomes. Figure 2.1 below shows how increasing income levels are tied to growth in services.

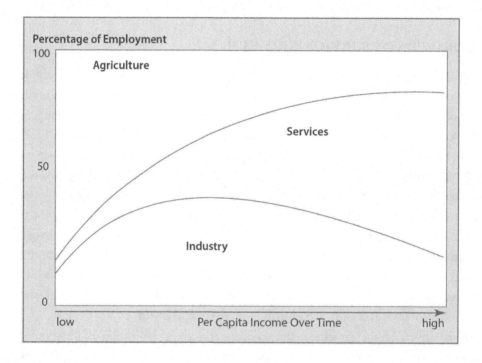

Figure 2.1: The changing structure of employment during economic development. Adapted from World Bank Group (2000: 51), Chapter IX—Growth of the Service Sector.

Helping to fuel service sector growth in developing countries is the increase in the global availability of services that were once thought to be "non-tradable," such as insurance, banking, education, and healthcare services. For example, people are now able to travel internationally to get the healthcare services and telemedicine is making it possible for advice and consultation services to be delivered at distance. There are now fewer restrictions on the access to services from both the developed and developing worlds allowing resources to flow more freely and opening up markets that were once out of reach to some. This is both enabling the rise of the service sector in the developing world and contributing to the movement of jobs, once thought to be geographically dependent, away from developed regions.

2.2   CHANGING SERVICE LANDSCAPE

Services enabled by digital technology are continuing to promote the expansion of the service economy, the diversity and variety of services, and the near ubiquitous access to many services. Products that were once sold as standalone commodities are now being offered for the services they enable. Information technology also is permitting the production of hyper-customized services which generates the opportunity to provide personalized services that match individual characteristics with custom offerings. For example, there are services that allow consumers to design their own jeans tailored to individual bodies and there are interior decorating services that match consumer tastes, budget, and existing floor plans with products that transform the look and functionality of people's homes. The forces of both standardization and customization are opening up possibilities for new services thus contributing to the growth and diversity of services.

2.2.1   PRODUCT-SERVICE SYSTEMS

Product-service systems, sometimes referred to as the servitization of products, typically are developed by product firms who provide services or solutions that supplement or replace their traditional product offerings. Recognizing that a product derives its value in use, these firms are focusing on the value derived from their product and exploring alternative ways of delivering that value as a service and charging for it. The strategy of bundling services with products involves selling services that are enabled by a product. For example, the purchase of a John Deere tractor enables access to services such as using GPS to automatically shift the steering to compensate for implement drift. John Deere offers this as a service that can be purchased as an add-on to the purchase of the tractor itself. Some firms are opting to retain ownership of the product, and only sell the service enabled by the product. A familiar example is renting a car from a rental agency for just when you need it and for the distances driven instead of buying a car. Newer business models use a Zipcar template where a stable of cars are a shared resource for a community and users check cars in and out for their personal use. Firms have been moving toward servitization of products for a number of reasons, but importantly they are realizing there is more profit to be made from selling services enabled by products than from the product itself. The product becomes a platform to deliver services.

With a somewhat different business model, companies like Salesforce.com, Intuit, and Adobe are providing software as a service (SaaS) where software applications are hosted by service providers and made available to customers over the Internet. So instead of buying software packages and/or licenses and installing them on proprietary hardware, firms are paying for the capabilities the software provides in increments that match their consumption needs. Not only can users access the applications when they need them, but the service provider takes responsibility for updates to the software and insures that all users have access to the same version of the software. The increasing availability of broadband services is supporting user access to these services from more locations around the world. Further accelerating the growth in SaaS is the emergence of Cloud infrastructures that that hold the promise to deliver IT enabled services ubiquitously and cost effectively.

2.2.2   PEER-TO-PEER AND SELF-SERVICE

In addition, services that were once marketed by for profit firms are now being proffered by individuals assembled through technology-enabled networks. These peer-to-peer and self-service offerings are bypassing traditional service providers and enabling people to procure services directly. In the first wave of self-service people were offered a kind of "help yourself" experience, as when hotel guests provide information directly via a touch-screen kiosk at check-in and—voila!—an electronic key is dispatched, saving the need for a desk clerk (Blomberg and Downs, 2014). More recently self-serve has expanded into a "help each other" model of self-service, exemplified by such start-up companies as Airbnb, Lyft, Zopa and Casserole (Blomberg and Downs, 2014). This new category of services mobilizes "peer-to-peer" networks of service providers as well as service recipients, where individuals develop new relationships to capital and to each other. For example, Airbnb allows individuals to offer spare rooms in their homes by becoming part of a network of "hotel" rooms where "under-utilized" assets are made available to guests who search, select, negotiate, pay for, and review the service. As Thackara (2005: 7) notes, "For more or less anything heavy and fixed, we don't have to own them—just know how and where to find them." And information technology is helping to make finding them a whole lot easier. These "help yourself" and "help each other" services, are having a significant effect on financial, tourism, transport, and even restaurant services.

Discussions of "helping each other" service offerings often juxtapose existing service providers such as taxi companies and hotel chains with new models that disrupt familiar ways of doing business. Long-standing working class jobs may be threatened by technologically savvy professionals who dabble in new realms of services. As real as these issues are they can deflect attention from other issues such as citizen action to redress inadequacies in government services. In effect, services are not provided *to* people as government entitlements, but *by* people to others who are bound through ties of reciprocity, often mediated by new technologies. Such collaborative services where people directly provide services such as childcare, meal preparation, rides to appointments, urban cleanup days, all services that governmental service agencies could and sometimes do provide, are made available by other citizens, neighbors, or loosely aligned extended "communities." These collaborative services raise many unresolved issues that are hotly debated regarding the proper role of government in people's lives and the importance of mechanisms to redistribute wealth.

Collaborative services are simultaneously innovative and traditional, and they suggest a need to rethink our concepts for understanding services. For example, one of the mechanisms used to connect people who have a need with those who can respond is *time banking* (Seyfang, 2004, 2006) where people invest their time with the expectation that they will be able to call upon others to provide services to them by similarly investing their time. Time banking has been characterized as "an alternative economic paradigm to exchanges of money…where everyone's contributions are valued on the same scale (time)… (Carroll, 2013: 137)." Time banking connects to a long history of neighbors helping neighbors such as the barn raising traditions of farmers where people would come together to erect a barn for a family in need. Unlike the time banks appearing today where technology makes it relatively easy to keep track of people's time investments, farmers kept only an informal accounting of the contribution of others often through stories and expectations of reciprocity. While time banking promises to add rigor and accountability to these more traditional models of neighborly reciprocity, more broadly collaborative services are changing—not always in benign ways—the way people connect to each other, to their possessions, to employment, and to their governments.

In addition, the expansion of self-service options in such fields as banking, retail, travel and tourism, tax preparation, music production, and home design are reconfiguring divisions of labor between humans, machines and capital. And the latter areas are contributing to a rise in the DIY (do it yourself) "culture" where what might be called professional amateurs or talented, knowledge-able laypeople are able to design and produce their own products and services. People are able to use new technologies to become creators of their own worlds by learning and applying practical skills creatively. Consumers become resources for the production of services and not just the loci of problems or opportunities to be addressed by services.

Some have argued that the combination of DIY culture and help each other self-service is leading to more communal and resource conserving lifestyles. Thackara (2005: 84) argues that "connecting people, resources, and places to each other in new combinations, on a real-time basis, delivers demand-responsive services that, when combined with location awareness and dynamic resource allocation, have the potential to reduce drastically the amount of hardware—from gadgets to buildings—that we need to function effectively." Clearly, the changing service landscape, in part enabled by technology, is reworking people's relations to one another and to their "possessions."

2.2.3   SERVICES AND THE INTERNET

The Internet has become increasingly important for the distribution of services, extending the reach of services into new and sometimes unforeseen markets and providing opportunities for a varied set of actors to become involved in economic activities. Older configurations of exclusively public or private concerns are yielding to more complex and idiosyncratic arrangements that bring together non-profits, public funding, foundation funding, exchange or barter, and donations. Notable here are crowdfunding firms like Kickstarter and Experiement.com, where people with projects—be they commercial, philanthropic, artistic, or scientific—appeal to the public for financial support with expectations of receiving some benefit in return, although not necessarily financial benefit to those contributing. Examples of projects that have been funded through crowd-funding include films, music, software, computer games, and scientific experiments.

Additionally, contributing to the growth in new services is the arrival of the *Internet of Things* where sensors send and receive information that connect people, places, and things to the Internet and to each other, thereby generating a subsequent explosion in the availability of the data streams created by these interconnections. Every day we learn of new apps that analyze these data to report on such things as buying habits, blood sugar levels, traffic congestion patterns, voting behaviors, parking space availability, cheap airline tickets, and the list goes on. Mobile devices such as smart phones and tablets give anytime access to these services and with embedded GPS chips further enabling location-aware services. Need a restaurant while traveling and there is an app to give recommendations for nearby places based on price, ambiance, or cuisine. Or looking for a taxi and an app will identify ones in the area. Or, if it is time to fill up your tank, there's an app to show you the least expensive gas stations in the area. Location-aware services are built on top of the increasing ubiquity of Internet connectivity.

2.2.4   MACHINE LABOR

Part of the story of the recent rise in services involves the emergence of new divisions of labor between humans and machines, some of which are dislocating workers and redefining human to human relations. Many of these digitally enabled services involve "hidden" machine-to-machine interactions that aggregate data from diverse sources, connect frequency data with geospatial displays, route users through task flows, and perform behind the scene calculations. Often unbeknownst to service recipients these digitized processes execute functions such as calculating, processing, sorting, and routing that trigger further actions making possible flight reservation confirmation and seat assignments, optimal routing of package delivery, real time notification of power outages, and more. These "smart" functions until recently were performed by a skilled human workforce—but efficiencies in cost and improvements in quality and reliability mean that data-driven algorithms are displacing people at an ever growing rate.

Reflecting on the growth in these technology enabled services, Arthur (2011: 2) worries that a "Second Economy" is emerging where human labor is displaced by machines and, "Business processes that once took place among human beings are now being executed electronically... in an unseen domain that is strictly digital." Worker dislocation as the result of automation is not new. Mechanized farming reduced the number of people needed on the farm and factory automation decreased manufacturing jobs. Services delivered through digital platforms and accessed via digital devices create dependencies on technology and change divisions of labor among service providers and recipients and among the human and non-human actors involved in delivering service.

These shifts in how services are constituted and delivered have a potentially dark side. For example, when technology is substituted for human labor in the service transaction as in bridge toll collection, not only is a job lost, but so to is the human connection with drivers some of whom take comfort in the daily social interchange as they commute. Likewise, some of these "hidden" service transactions conceal the exercise of power by one group over another as when Facebook manipulates the page views of users to assess their emotive responses and affect their behavior. We are not suggesting that more traditional services have no dark side or that they do not benefit some at the expense of others, only that we need to look beyond the hype of these new service relationships and explore the distinct meanings and experiences they have for differently positioned people.

2.2.5   WORK AND THE SERVICE ECONOMY

As services have come to dominate the world economy there is a heightened interest in how the service economy is affecting the nature of work and the workers employed in the service sector. The industrial model where standardization, mechanization, and optimization are viewed as keys to economic success may not be as applicable in a world where knowledge and creativity provide competitive advantage for firms and workers alike. The argument rests on the view that a source of economic value in the service economy derives from the skills, experiences, and capabilities of workers and not primarily from fixed assets or access to raw materials as is the case in a goods dominate economy.

However, we should note that alongside the increase in demand for workers in the so-called knowledge-intensive service sector (e.g., science and technology, art and design, culture, and entertainment, business and finance) is another group of service workers who work at relatively low-paying jobs in the retail, food service, janitorial, and personal care sectors (Herzenberg et al., 1998). These broad differences in the work of service providers reflect competing views of the rise of the service economy, one rather optimistic that focuses on knowledge-intensive and high-skilled labor (Frenkel et al., 1999) and the other that portrays service sector jobs as menial, gendered, and amenable to offshoring (Rothman, 1998). These two diverse realities of service sector jobs may be responsible in part for creating new social, economic, and cultural divides between those who are employed in service jobs requiring high levels of education and professional certification and those who work in low-paying jobs with few barriers to entry (Blomberg, 2010).

However, this story continues to evolve and as we noted increasingly the jobs of highly educated workers are changing, and in some instances are being replaced and outsourced, because of new technologies. For example, college lectures can be viewed by thousands of students distributed across the globe through MOOCs and medical images can be "read" by image processing machines and reviewed at distance by technicians, leaving only the anomalies for the attention of highly trained doctors. This is not a completely new phenomenon as automation has been changing the landscape of work for decades. But it seems fewer and fewer workers are immune from the threat of job displacement which likely in part is to blame for the recent U.S. jobless recovery.

2.3   SERVICE WORLDS

The developments we described in this chapter demonstrate that simply contrasting services with manufacturing or high- and low-wage service sector employment oversimplifies the complexity and ambiguity of services and the extent to which they are integrated into the fabric of contemporary life. Services can replace activities we already perform, such as when we use a restaurant to cook our meals or an accountant to prepare our taxes, but they increasingly exist in bundles that create and support entirely new kinds of activities, often in ways we barely comprehend. It is for these reasons that we speak not just of services, but of service *worlds* that not only fit into society but that transform it. Bryson et al. (2004) use the concept of service worlds to emphasize the ways that services are integral components of production processes. We expand the concept by using it to draw attention to how services contribute to the organization of society. For example, services require the social production of people who need and value them, just as services may alter existing social relations and values; restaurants may affect the valuing of "home-cooked meals" or the reciprocity among kinfolk. By addressing service worlds we acknowledge that something disjunctive and significant is afoot, and it takes forms that can render familiar vocabularies inadequate. Yet we also argue that services have always been a part of the organization of social life, a claim we explore in Chapter 3.

It is difficult to imagine how we can understand contemporary social life without understanding the service worlds that flow into and out of the everyday lives of people. Just as an earlier generation of anthropologists who were trained to study bands, tribes, and chiefdoms expanded their focus to include the study industrial societies, so too there are many reasons to turn our gaze to service worlds. Anthropology as the discipline of the human experience cannot ignore these changes. They constitute a shift in how people relate and interact, what they value or think is part of the good life, and even what it means to be a person. As such, because services are constituted through human interaction and performance and because they represent economic changes that have deep social ramifications, service worlds provide a rich arena for research and intervention, one that we cannot afford to ignore and one that begs for the holistic lens provided by anthropology.

CHAPTER 3

The Human Condition

Just as our initial encounter with service worlds was grounded in our training and experiences as anthropologists, we found ourselves inquiring about the place of those worlds in the broader account of humanity that anthropology provides. Services and their worlds seemed new and exotic to a couple of anthropologists originally trained in analyzing preliterate societies and treating diverse cultures past and present as part of the human experience. We wondered how our backgrounds might contribute to understanding contemporary service worlds and how they might evolve in the future. Much of the discourse about services that we encountered on our journey seemed somehow familiar with the talk of service encounters and performances and our conversations often turned to bemusement about what distinctions were being called out in the discourse on the ubiquity of services.

3.1 THE SERVICE WORLD OF THE TROBRIAND ISLANDERS

Consider the anthropological classic study of the Trobriand Islanders made famous by Bronislaw Malinowski's accounts of the *kula* ring (Malinowski, 1922). The Trobriand Islands lie off the eastern coast of New Guinea and yams are the primary crop; their great advantage in a tropical climate is that they can be stored for months. They are grown by gardening teams comprised of kinship groups and although families cultivate and devour their own yams, they also grow them in dedicated production for exchange with other groups. Yam production exceeds the nutritional needs of households and about half goes to the households of a man's sisters. Generosity here translates into higher prestige and yams of distinction are displayed in publicly visible yam houses as symbols of wealth and esteem. Many such yams ultimately are left to rot, testimony to the wealth of their owners.

Yams are much more than food. Uncooked yams are effectively capital that can be invested in social networks; cooked ones can only be eaten. Materials planted in the exchange plots are provided by the recipients of yams from the previous year so that in effect the yams from an exchange garden give tangible expression to labor. These exchanges convert an ordinary tuber into social status and, significantly, the exchange gardens are the sites of the garden magician's efforts because these yams maintain delicate social relations, while subsistence yams are merely food that sustains individuals but do not connect the owner to larger social networks. Trobriand Islanders indeed grow and process yams, but so too do yams play a part in creating and transforming social relationships, and in creating Trobriand identities.

Yams move from place to place through different modes of exchange. *Kabutu* consists of labor drawn from kin, in-laws, and neighbors to build houses or other structures. Leaders with surplus yams use them to mobilize labor for projects that result in increased prestige for everyone involved. *Sagali* involves giving away food as an accompaniment to a ceremony or social occasion. *Pokala* are presentations from juniors or subordinates to their superordinates for future claims on resources. They can be moved to secure political advantage, validate rights to inheritance, or provide tribute to leaders. Acceptance of the presentations by higher ranked individuals obligates them to subordinates. Women participate in similar exchanges built upon mortuary rituals undertaken when a member of a woman's clan dies: grass skirts and banana leaf bundles are the objects of exchange.

Kabutu, *sagali*, and *pokala* demonstrate that uncooked yams are a form of capital that can be invested for future benefit. Once cooked, they must soon be consumed and are no longer capital. They publicly proclaim status and power, while the rituals of exchange bind individuals together. In a sense yams nourish individuals *and* their social relationships, largely through the provision of services.

The Trobriand Islands lack many resources, requiring both trade among areas of the islands as well as through long-distance canoe voyages. The islands are part of the larger *kula* ring of ceremonial exchange among islands strung out around several hundred kilometers of ocean. *Soulava*, long necklaces of shell disks, move clockwise around the ring and are exchanged for white *mwali* arm shells that are moving counterclockwise. The *kula* exchanges occur between trading partners without bargaining, although there is maneuvering to obtain the most prestigious *soulava* and *mwali* in order to increase individuals' prestige and power. While the *kula* ring may seem dramatic and exotic, especially since it involves risky voyages for ritual objects, it is accompanied by *gimwali* bargaining for everyday goods following market logic. Pottery, rattan, stones, and other subsistence resources are the accompaniment to *kula* exchanges, resulting in a distributed peace pact among the societies of different islands.

The experiences of a Trobriand Island man just returning from a *kula* ring voyage might seem far removed from those of most readers of this book, but we suggest there are important commonalities. The Trobriand Island economy engages individuals and collectivities in providing services, even if they are not described in the language of contemporary service worlds. Social institutions provide the contexts that make services comprehensible and valuable to people. Members of a society typically take for granted the value and even necessity of specific services that may appear extraordinarily strange to outsiders. This is no less true for contemporary iPad toting knowledge workers confronted by the Trobriand Islanders than it would be for Islanders gazing at the array of services available in postindustrial societies. Even the language we used to understand the Trobriand Islands is familiar, for we speak of investment, accountability, performance, and the role of transformations in organizing social life.

At the outset then, as anthropologists we were preconditioned to see continuities between contemporary services that are often presented as markers of a new sort of society. In fact, we felt that the "exotic" societies of the anthropological record may even help us think differently about service worlds. If the Trobriand Islanders had, as we felt, a service economy it was one in which ceremony, ritual, and cosmology contributed significantly to the necessity and value of services; concepts like efficiency, productivity, and return on investment that are taken for granted as essential measures of services fail to capture important characteristics of the services rendered. Instead, the Trobriand Islanders had created multiple spheres of exchange, each following distinct rules: there was no single over-arching calculus of value and some kinds of exchanges were incommensurate with others. Likewise, the services we saw were not planned, implemented, and maintained, and they certainly lacked the hand of the designer or the expert practitioner who could describe them as well-bounded whole systems. They were foundational to the survival of the Islanders as people with a distinct identity that was nonetheless fuzzy at the edges where they collided and conspired with people from other societies.

Service worlds are often starkly contrasted with industrialization and the manufacture of goods. In fact, the rise of the service sector is often presented as a transformation that is sweeping away all that came before. We argue here that services broadly construed have always characterized societies and contemporary service worlds are as old as the species. From this perspective, humans have always inhabited service worlds, although they have taken very different forms throughout human history and in different parts of the world. Our interest is in the ways people have served one another quite apart from those societies today where distinctive service sectors are called out.

3.2   HUMAN SOCIETIES THROUGHOUT HISTORY

Our grounding of service worlds in the human condition is undertaken not as an academic exercise, but as a practical one. By developing a broader understanding of services, one that sees them integral to societies including non-western ones, we expand the scope of alternatives to draw upon when envisioning new services and the consequences they may have for how people live their lives. While services are often described as providing for human betterment, they also can detract from how people engage with one another. In this chapter we explore what is lost (and gained) when a simple "service logic" borne of the modern age shapes how we engage and serve each other.

We begin by looking at the development of human societies as reflected in the archaeological and ethnographic records to find evidence of services. Part of the human condition, and a basic way we adapt, involves providing services to one another even if we do not describe these interactions as services or as part of a service sector. This is a story that reflects local circumstances and has unfolded in myriad ways that cannot be recounted in detail. But it suggests that services are not quite as new and distinctive as we often tell ourselves. We summarize below some broad patterns of this development without claiming that it provides the master narrative of all societies or that it is not without inconsistencies and exceptions (Johnson and Earle, 1987).

Band-level societies, such as the San of southern Africa or the Shoshone of the American Great Basin, were organized around families. For these societies, a recurring challenge was that of access to food, especially to mitigate the effects of fluctuating supplies of animals and plants. Risk management was critical to survival and it was performed among families via their mobility, and through information exchange and reciprocity based on sharing resources. A resulting tension was between the benefits of cooperation and the potential for conflict as individuals lived even temporarily in close proximity. Domestication of plants and animals intensified food production through horticultural gardens and agricultural fields while simultaneously exacerbating the risks inherent to settled populations which were often in competition for the same productive plots of land. These societies developed sodalities such as healing or military societies that cut across discrete family groups and allowed some integration beyond that provided by ties of inter-group marriage. Sodalities served more to temper conflicts than to provide for unitary political action. Leaders today referred to as Big Men emerged as skilled negotiators, marriage brokers, and organizers of large-scale ceremonies; simultaneously, family autonomy became restricted by collective obligations. Indeed, a typical task of tribal leaders was to mobilize the production of surplus food among their groups in order to support ceremonies.

Chiefdoms are marked by unequal access to the means of production that characterized a society: social stratification and inequality commences. Large-scale technological productions such as irrigation canals, terracing, drainage, fishing structures, and food storage begin, further intensifying productivity. In effect, chiefdoms provided a mechanism to invest surpluses in order to buffer future scarcity. Trade, both local and long-distance, grew in importance resulting in a symbiosis of very different kinds of producers. This increased integration of larger populations also resulted in warfare, public ceremonials to remind the populace of its common interests, and ways to manage or account for ownership of property and obligations to contribute to the collective well-being. Larger populations were desirable in order to intensify further production and defend territories, but they brought with them increased potential for conflict and drove the need for means to control it.

Finally, early states such as in Mesopotamia and Egypt were organized around the control of territory through military forces, bureaucracies to manage income and expenditures, and religions to sanctify rule. These are societies that produced luxury goods to demarcate elite social status and public monuments to attract and motivate a citizenry. Population densities typically increased through further intensification brought about by large-scale public works that mobilized legions of workers to produce and maintain them. The pattern was typically to incorporate new populations by offering an imposed peace in exchange for labor; the formation of the Inca Empire was exemplary. Finance systems required record keeping and specialized craft were detached from local communities; they marked regional elites and because they were high-value and low-bulk they were ideal for long distance trade.

3.3   SERVICES AND THE HUMAN CONDITION

The preceding discussion merely outlines a pattern with numerous local manifestations and exceptions, but we see in it the recurrence of risk management, warfare and conflict management, technologies of increasing scale that improve productivity, and trade. This pattern has lessons for understanding services.

First, in fulfilling a mission to understand diverse cultures anthropologists often emphasize differences among them. But equally important are the similarities that establish a common humanity and so it is not surprising that much of the tale we have recounted should sound familiar. True, the customs and fashions, artifacts, and cosmologies of other societies often seem exotic from the vantage point of another society and the lifestyles of contemporary denizens of industrial and post-industrial societies differ in important ways from those of earlier societies. But concepts like risk and conflict management, accounting and investment, and the role of public spectacle suggest a deeper similarity. Societies represented as dominated by the service sector *are* distinctive, but they are not so different as to be populated by an entirely new kind of people. Today's health care debates and ruminations about the impact of high-tech may contrast with debates of even a few years ago, but they really are not entirely new. Shamans and herbalists have long provided healing services and artisans have offered services that alter the material world such as boat making, decorative painting, or flint knapping. While service worlds are seemingly new, they are also firmly grounded in a human past where services were fundamental to human adaptation and to the organization of societies. We see them as both less distinctive than perhaps other scholars and also as more important to the very basis of what it is to be human.

Second, we also can see much of the development of social groups above the level of the family as providing services that would not otherwise be available. They, in fact, develop at the limits of family agency. They are not simply about the production of artifacts in pre-capitalist societies, but about the transformations that also characterize contemporary service worlds. This is not to argue that societies of the past are the same as those of the present. But the contrast that has been drawn between economies dominated by manufacturing and the new service economies masks a deeper continuity with how humans adapt. This allows us to appreciate that industrial manufacturing is not a prerequisite for services and that services are not only a feature of capitalist economies or subject to measurement only by concepts such as efficiency and return on investment. Likewise, we see that services can be inferred from the archaeological record, suggesting that they are central to how people survived in part by creating a built environment. While services have been linked to sustainability due to their supposed immateriality as contrasted with manufacturing, our temporal view of services suggests that they have always been and are today preserved through material embodiments.

Finally, even a cursory look at the human past and contemporary societies reveals a world characterized by rich and complex services long before services were placed in an economic sector and deemed the object of design and marketing by professionals. By grounding services in what we are calling the human condition they are revealed to be multifaceted. Services can be at the heart of dynasties and empires based on the capacity to shape the everyday lives of people and at times to control entire populations. Sometimes these services may seem benign or beneficial, such as healing, regulating weights and measures, or insuring property rights, but they may on occasion undermine democratic values and self-determination. Services are varied and far from uniformly beneficial for one and all, for they can simultaneously be about abstract transformations, constructing material embodiments, personal liberation, social justice, and the exercise of power by large organizations or the state.

3.4   FAMILIES

The integral place of services in social life over time can be explored by further looking at the institutions of the family. Throughout human history, families endured, but they became increasingly dependent on external resources and subject to influence and control from afar. Examining activities that occur in families reveals a great variety of services that families have performed, although they typically are not described in the contemporary language of services. In this sense there are many services that are hidden in plain view. Harrell (1997) provides a glimpse into this world of services through the familiar portal of the family. He asks us to consider how the activities occurring in families have changed under modernity. His analysis shows that many of the services that were once performed in families are no longer performed there or at least they are also performed in other settings.

Throughout human history families have been responsible for procuring the materials necessary for subsistence or luxury consumption. The family performs these services in two ways; as the work group or the unit of procurement and as the unit of consumption. There has been a decline in the role of families as work groups as public companies and government agencies increase in scale. This has resulted in a decline in intergenerational interdependencies within the family. Children have less value for security in old age or as sources of labor for the family estate. Now employment and salary allows people to procure goods and services without being in a family as long as they have access to employment opportunities.

Along with the role of families in procuring goods, they also have been involved in the processing of goods often through gender- and age-based divisions of labor. Processing activities include (among others) cleaning, food preparation, and household repairs. Over the years there has been a reduction in the time and changes in the skills needed to process goods due to changes in technologies and products such as washing machines and driers, permanent press fabrics, and frozen and take-out dinners. At the same time new standards of living that emphasize the dwelling as a site for aesthetic appreciation and rising standards of cleanliness above the simple requirement for shelter have increased the scope of housework and led to greater demand to purchase the services of house cleaners, window washers, pool men, and gardeners. People continue to organize themselves in families and households so they can lay claim to processing work even though it is increasingly done for pay.

Families also have provided representation for family members in public politics and community rituals. The family managed its place in the public sphere, which had consequences for individual members. Today the rise of the state and the decline of intermediaries between the state and individuals reduce the dependence families and individuals have on religious and other community institutions. The individual directly interfaces with the state through citizenship rights and responsibilities limiting the role of the family as a spokesperson for its members in property transactions or criminal transgressions. These issues are now mediated by laws. Individuals may hire accountants and lawyers and other service providers to shape their public image and navigate community expectations. Similarly, families have provided services that enabled their members to participate in public activities of politics, adjudication, and ritual. They mustered the resources of time, effort, and money so family members could advance within society. Modernity has allowed individuals to advance through their own individual effort, where education and personal income are used to advance careers although family advantage shapes access to these resources. Harrell (1997) in the end argues that as the role of families in the procurement and processing of goods, in the representation of the family in the public sphere, and in advancing family members status in society has diminished, the primary *remaining* service provided by families is the emotional warmth and comfort they offer while acknowledging that not all families perform this service.

Like Johnson and Earle (1987), Harrell bases his account of the family as a distinguishing human institution by assembling a breadth of comparative data and his goal is to delineate the broadest patterns in that data. He makes no claims to have discovered the universal mechanisms of the human family, but once again there are lessons to be learned for anyone interested in service worlds and in designing services.

3.5   MEANING AND VALUE OF SERVICES

Services have always been embedded in social institutions that give them meaning and even allow people to recognize them as something of value. But they are not simply *in* an institution for they cut across the wider practices of society often in unpredictable ways. Anthropologists are perhaps the ultimate holistic disciplinarians in that they are trained to unravel the connections between what at first might seem like disconnected facets of a culture. They think, for example, that family cannot be comprehended without exploring how it is connected to ecological adaptation, macro and micro economics, large- and small scale-politics, spirituality and artistic expression, to name just a few domains. In the past, as now, people live in service worlds where services are seldom clearly bounded, but bleed into each other. Universities that provide the service of education may simultaneously be providing dating services by bringing together potential romantic partners under conditions in which they can judge one another's career potentials. In spite of the professor's goals, students may judge a course they failed as successful if they find the right partner. The anthropological record teaches us to be suspicious of tidily bounded entities that are viewed the same by everyone, and to look for differences and privileges in perspective that shape how problems and solutions, and costs and benefits are defined. Harrell's families, as he would be the first to agree, are seen differently by their members: a family may be a site of shelter from a harsh world or the site of inequality and even fear. While many have noted that services cannot be described apart from or prior to their use by participants, in fact, the fragments of what may be identified as a single service reflect the intentions and actions of multiple participants.

Our review of families also reminds us that value infuses all that people do rendering it irreducible to economic value propositions. As we examine the human condition we realize that services cannot be described fully as "value propositions" expressed as economic transactions between individuals or firms, but instead services make sense and are comprehensible only in particular social contexts. To understand the interactions, transformations, meanings, and exchanges that characterize services accordingly requires studying them in the variety of social contexts where they are performed through people's day-to-day practices. By doing so, we argue, some of the assumptions and limitations of contemporary conceptualizations of services are overcome and new directions for how we might affect service worlds are identified.

Furthermore, the perspectives of the family members and others involved in services matter since it is they who define the service, the interactions and encounters that characterize it, and the value that it creates—or not. This means that it is both unnecessary and unwise to insist upon a single definition for a service, one agreed upon by all participants. A rich literature in the social construction of technologies (Bijker et al., 1987; Bijker and Law, 1992; Blomberg, 1988; Kline and Pinch, 1996; MacKenzie and Wajcman, 1999; Pinch and Bijker, 1984) has revealed how, despite the intentions of designers, their creations are assimilated and reworked by users often in unanticipated ways. Kline and Pinch (1996: 765) note that, "...the use of an artefact or system has not only resulted in unforeseen consequences, but that users have helped to shape the artefact or system itself." Bricks may have been designed to be mortared into walls, but generations of students have stacked them to support wobbly bookshelves. Designers may decry these "repurposings" but they are nonetheless ubiquitous—so too with services. For example, middle school students in Hong Kong turn McDonald's fast food restaurants into places for studying and gossiping (Watson, 1997) and late-night transit buses in Silicon Valley become overnight housing for the poor and dispossessed (CBS Radio Inc., 2013). There is no privileged definition of the constituents of a service and participants will make of them what they will, despite pleas for consensus; a lesson that service designers can ill-afford to neglect.

Our argument in this chapter has been that, in order to understand services, we must examine the human past and the incredible variety of societies. Such an examination is not, we suggest, an exercise in anthropological romanticism or nostalgia, for services today take us to fundamental questions about ownership and the control of resources that challenge conventional notions of how people can and should interact with each other and transact exchanges.

CHAPTER 4

Service Concepts

As we continued our journey we began to see how contemporary services represent more continuity with the human condition than the scholarly literature sometimes suggests. Moreover the growing importance of services in the world economy was stimulating scholarship that described and analyzed services in order to understand, modify, and create them. Scholars and practitioners were developing service concepts in their quest to describe, engage, and ultimately have an impact on contemporary service worlds. We also observed that many services were vernacular in that they were assembled by ordinary folk who drew upon their understandings and experiences for getting things done. For example, someone opening a diner in the 1950s in a small town bisected by a lonely highway was probably drawing upon beliefs about time, distance, hunger, and domesticity. The location, marketing messages, branding, or menu options were not informed by formal ways of knowing, but nonetheless new services were emerging in response to changes in travel and the movement of goods along newly created roadways. We were interested in understanding how service concepts might aid in our understanding of the services we encountered and ultimately in designing and managing them. As such, we were compelled to explore the connections between the concepts used to describe services and those that might inform an anthropology of services and our practice approach to designing services.

In part, due to the growth in the service sector in the economies of the world, interest was growing in applying scientific ways of knowing to services so that businesses, not-for-profit organizations, and governments could more systematically innovate within this sector. Building on previous research on services, primarily from the field of marketing (Grönroos, 1984; Gummesson, 1987; Lovelock and Wirtz, 2004; Oliver et al., 1997; Teboul, 2006;), new efforts were emerging that applied engineering and management disciplines to understand and gain more control over services and the service economy. In this regard a new field of research was being defined called SSME (Service Science, Management, and Engineering) that aimed at creating a "science of service" (Spohrer and Maglio, 2008; 2010). In the decade since the first SSME paper was published (Maglio et al., 2006) connections and productive collaborations with the service marketing community (Maglio et al., 2009; Vargo and Lusch, 2011; Vargo et al., 2008) also developed with the joint aim of advancing the science of service.

The scholarship on services continues to evolve rapidly and its nomenclature has not always been consistent. But service scientists have been developing a set of concepts and a vocabulary for systematically inquiring about services motivated in part by the acknowledgement that science proceeds by developing and refining concepts to describe the phenomena of interest. In this regard, Saco and Gonsalves (2008:10) have argued for the "...need to codify the language and artifacts of the world of service...create an entirely new language of service," as distinct from the language of manufacturing in order to allow scholars who approach services from different standpoints to collaborate.

While a common language does not by itself resolve disciplinary differences in knowledge claims and know-how, the hope is that systematic, agreed upon approaches to describing services will enable us to transcend the limits of locally grounded descriptions, facilitate the design of more complex services, and ultimately introduce greater predictability into service outcomes. Our interest is to explore how particular ways of conceptualizing services have consequences for how we understand and engage with contemporary service worlds. Service science concepts are not only of interest for how they help us understand services, but also as expressions of the worldview of a community of practice. These concepts do not just describe services, but they simultaneously define the world as a particular place with attendant opportunities and constraints on our ability to intervene. We believe that an assessment of service concepts, one that considers the assumptions and modes of thought that they rest upon, can deepen and enrich our understanding of service worlds. We are not arguing for or against a new language of services, but instead we want to acknowledge that the concepts used to describe service worlds are enormously consequential for our practices as researchers and designers. An anthropology of services attunes us to the role service concepts play in defining the ways we intervene in service worlds and the possibilities for a practice approach to designing services.

We focus here on three overarching concepts used to describe and understand contemporary services: services, service encounters, and service systems. The concept of *services* is foundational and without it the notion of a service science makes little sense. The concept of *service encounter* captures the engagement of people with services through interactions, performances, and transactions. It is through encounters between service providers and recipients that services are realized. *Service systems* expresses the view that services draw together heterogeneous elements and coordinates them as a system. Service systems may be invisible to the users of a service, but they support service encounters by mustering information, spaces and artifacts, participants, and flows of capital to ensure that the service can provide its essential transformations over time.

4.1   SERVICES

The concept of service can be vexing precisely because it seems so obvious and familiar; the concept is widely used by scholars and ordinary folk alike. The usage by scholars naturally introduces a specialized vocabulary that might seem alien to other audiences, a common property of scholarly discourse in most fields. While there are numerous definitions of services, early definitions almost always make reference to how services differ from goods. It is said that services provide intangible benefits which, through some form of exchange, satisfy identified needs (Zeithaml, 1981; Rushton and Carson, 1989; Berry, 1995). Also emphasized is the difficulty of separating service production from consumption, noting that services are produced as they are consumed (Zeithaml et al., 1985). For example, a tax preparation service is consumed at the point the taxes are prepared which requires input from the taxpayer. An implication is that services cannot be inventoried or stored since they do not exist until they are consumed. Finally, definitions stress the difficulty of standardizing services because of the heterogeneity of service recipients who are themselves involved in producing the service. For instance, the service provided by a financial advisor to someone who is just beginning to make investments is likely quite different from the service received by someone with multiple investments and nearing retirement. The financial advisor's expertise is in part to know what strategies are relevant to which clients. Likewise, the clients' knowledge will affect what they are able to make of the advisor's recommendations and accordingly, the nature of the service. Lovelock and Gummesson (2004) argue for the importance of distinguishing between heterogeneity that is the result of differences in clients' skills, knowledge, and experience from that which follows from differences among providers since the latter sources of variability can be mitigated to some degree through standardization and automation.

The characteristics of intangibility, heterogeneity, inseparability of production and consumption, and perishability (or IHIP) were long used in service marketing to distinguish services from goods (Zeithaml et al., 1985; Edgett and Parkinson, 1993). However, more recently, scholars have challenged these as defining characteristics of services, pointing out that they are not uniformly applicable to all services and are also attributable to some manufactured goods (Lovelock and Gummesson, 2004). Lovelock and Gummesson (2004) go on to suggest that a more useful distinction between services and goods is that services cannot be owned. That is services give customers the right of access to objects and to the labor and expertise of others. In this way a car is rented, a golf course is accessed, or the skill of a fitness instructor is obtained for a specified period of time. This definition is suggestive of our earlier discussion of the servitization of tangible products where ownership of things is secondary to the value that can be obtained from their use and/or derivative outputs (e.g., data from Google searches).

In addition, scholars have been critical of the IHIP characteristics of services that define services for what they are *not*—not tangible, standardized, first produced and then consumed, nor able to be inventoried. In recent years, efforts have been directed at defining services for what they are, not as juxtaposed to products. At the forefront of these efforts have been the work of Teboul (2006) and Vargo and Lusch (2004a, 2006). Teboul focuses his characterization of services on the transformations that services bring about to people and objects. For example, educational services hold the promise of making people more informed or skilled and laundry services transform clothes from dirty to clean. Vargo and Lusch (2008b: 26) stress that service, "...the application of specialized competences (operant resources—knowledge and skills), through deeds, processes, and performances for the benefit of another entity or the entity itself." Their emphasis is on what it takes to bring about transformations or in their vocabulary the "benefit" realized by an entity, be that a person or thing.

The irony for us is that the scholarly discourse about services defines services as an analytically distinct phenomenon of interest and service science as a distinct field of scholarship. But by abstracting services and by developing a specialized vocabulary to describe them, scholars are framing questions that in the end can only be answered by exploring the social context within which services make sense. In doing so notions that effectively resituate services within a larger sociocultural context are introduced. This is a place where the social sciences, such as anthropology, have long dwelled. We explore two such sets of issues—co-production and co-creation and service dominate logic.

4.1.1   CO-PRODUCTION AND CO-CREATION

As mentioned, one of the fundamental characteristics that has been used to distinguish services from products is the inseparability of service production and consumption. Zeithaml et al. (1985) argue that because services are simultaneously produced and consumed, they position the service recipient in an intimate relationship with the production process. In essence, service recipients become co-producers of the service as they mobilize knowledge and other resources in the service process. Later, Vargo and Lusch (2008a) made a distinction between co-production and co-creation, where co-creation is not focused on the production process, *per se*, stressing instead the value created in the service exchange for both provider and recipient. Customers, or service recipients, are viewed as the co-creators of value because their actions affect service outcomes and the attending value received by both provider and recipient. More recently, Vargo and Lusch (2011: 2) have stressed the interchangeability of provider and recipient roles, choosing to use the "more abstract designation" of actor-to-actor relationships. Grönroos (2011) has argued for the need to distinguish the value-in-use that the customer receives from the value that is enabled by the activities of providers that occur prior to or outside the use situation. He (2011:14) defines service as "value-creating support to another party's practices" which alleviates that party from having to perform certain tasks or helps them accomplish things they would not otherwise be able to do. He notes that an all-encompassing notion of service value must include the potential value generated in "design, development and manufacturing of resources, and back office processes" (2011; 8). In this sense, service recipients, along with providers, are both co-producers and co-creators of service and service value.

Precisely because services are co-productions in which value is created in and through interactions between provider and recipient, people must learn how to participate appropriately in service encounters by identifying and ascribing meaning to characteristic elements of the service. Part of being a competent member of society involves learning how to perform, including in the context of a service exchange. This process can unfold smoothly and with minimal disruption as when service participants assume familiar roles. But it can also be complex and contested, as when members of post-colonial societies are taught how to present themselves as good hosts for different kinds of tourists (Hall and Tucker, 2004) or when Latinos are trained to perform as Benihana "Japanese" chefs (Hirose and Kei-Ho Pih, 2011). As these examples attest, the "co" in co-production and co-creation often conceals the complexity of provider-recipient relations, including the unequal character of some of these partnerships.

Campbell, et al. (2012) in their discussion of how resources are conceptualized in the context of service-dominate-logic also caution that too narrow a focus on the value received by the "beneficiaries" of a service, can fail to capture how others may be harmed in the process. Borrowing their example, consumption of shark fins may provide great value for those who enjoy this delicacy, but in the process those who value preservation of sharks or have broader ecological concerns may suffer and in essence have value taken away. In this sense there may be value in non-use as in the case of shark fins.

An anthropology of services and a practice approach to intervening in service worlds stresses the importance of acknowledging these complexities in order to pursue societal, community, or even larger business ecosystem aims that go beyond the immediate outcome or value delivered through the service. Because services are enacted by people who participate in different institutions and lifestyles, and who thus bring different expectations to the service encounter, their relationships to the service process are never singular or constant. Consensus among participants about a service is often impossible and unnecessary to achieve. Thus, co-production and co-creation introduce a significant element of unpredictability into service outcomes (Bitner et al., 1997; Grönroos, 2011) and the decidedly variable value delivered. This points to the need to accept a level of openness and modesty in our professional ability to define services, or to design them, without consideration given to the broader and diverse social contexts of actors in the service exchange.

4.1.2   SERVICE DOMINATE LOGIC

Vargo and Lusch (2004b) introduced the notion of service-dominant logic as an alternative to the goods-dominant focus that placed services in a secondary role to tangible products. They defined service as the process of doing something for someone, shifting focus to processes and arguing that service is the fundamental unit of exchange. As such, goods should be viewed as enablers of services, such as automobiles facilitating the service of transportation. Furthermore, they argued that "things" could only be valued in use, meaning that goods too had to be enacted for their value to be realized. The value of an automobile was realized when it was used to get from point A to B and this involved a driver, possible passengers and cargo, the roadway, other cars, and so on.

The notion of service-dominate logic has stimulated much debate, particularly in light of its larger ambition to become a "revised theory of economics and society" (Vargo and Lusch 2008a). Scholars have returned to earlier writings in service marketing and economics to trace the emergence of notions of a *service logic* with implications for economic and business development (Grönroos, 2006, 2011; Gummesson, 2008). The concept has enjoyed a number of refinements over the years since the initial Vargo and Lusch publications in 2004 and to some degree consensus has been reached that the strong disjuncture between goods (material things) and services (intangible things) cannot be and should not be promulgated.

This conclusion is not particularly surprising to anthropologists who have long understood that people have always lived in social worlds that are simultaneously material and immaterial and they have always been entangled with each other in creating things, ideas, and interactions. It is only recently that the things we make and do together have been framed as goods or services, and together as products. A nomadic hunter living in the desert of southern Africa plays a flute crafted by his uncle to entertain families gathered around the camp fire after a successful hunt (Lee, 1979). This scene could be described as constituted by services; the service of the uncle who designed and built the flute, the service of the musician who performed under the evening sky, the service of the hunters who killed the game and butchered it for distribution. This scene also could be described in terms of the goods that were exchanged, the flute perhaps given to the nephew at a key juncture in his life; the meat allocated according to long standing rules.

Just as arguments for co-production and co-creation blur the line between services as discrete domains of activities and the larger society, service-dominant logic dissolves the boundary between goods as obviously material and services as equally obvious abstractions. Reflecting on the materiality of services also exposes all the material resources that are marshaled and consumed so that a service that may seem primarily information-based is available to recipients. For example, the ability to "surf" the web, compare prices, and purchase something is only possible because cables were laid across the oceans, devices such as PCs, tablets, and smartphones were produced, ships were manufactured to bring the goods to the shopper, vast "server farms" were set-up and managed to store information about products, and so on. While it may seem like the service of Internet shopping is primarily about manipulating information, in fact many material resources were and continue to be consumed in the process. In addition, left out of the equation is the labor that went into making the products, bringing them to market, and to the shopper's doorstep. Far from being immaterial services implicate and require the assembly of human and non-human resources.

The record of the human past and of those contemporary societies that participate only peripherally in what we refer to as the service economy remind us that the human experience and the meanings (and value) we derive from our interactions with each other and with things depend on specific social and material arrangements (Suchman, 2007). Distinctions such as between goods and services are always drawn within specific communities of practice and are not necessarily salient for the people whose daily lives we study and attempt to better through purposeful interventions. Scholars create dichotomies for their own purposes and then face the challenge of reconciling them in relation to the realities of people's everyday lives. The irony is that by developing specialized vocabularies we are ultimately led back into the broader record of human achievement where matter, energy, and information have long been elements of social practices.

4.2   SERVICE ENCOUNTER

The notion of a service encounter is at the center of how services are made tangible or manifested. Shostack (1985: 243) defines a service encounter as "a period of time during which a consumer directly interacts with a service." These interactions include those with physical facilities such as places and artifacts as well as with the people involved in delivering the service. Clatworthy (2011) adds that, "Each time a person relates to, or interacts with, a touch-point, they have a service-encounter."

The concept of service encounter is seemingly simple, but it belies the complexity of some encounters and also their variability. An encounter with a massage therapist, involving bodily contact and ongoing communication about appropriate levels of pain, is notably different from an encounter with a service technician located many time zones away occurring through a chat line. Similarly an encounter with a physician diagnosing a persistent cough is markedly different than an encounter between a global sales team of a technology company and members of a potential client's IT department which likely involves multiple people with differing roles and expertise. Furthermore, determining the boundaries of an encounter—when it begins and ends—may not always be that straightforward. For example, an interaction with a gardener who regularly maintains the yard of a client may include an initial greeting, then later a reminder to check the irrigation system at which time an invoice is presented. Is this a single encounter, two encounters occurring at two different times, or three where the reminder to check the irrigation system and the payment for services are treated as separate encounters? On other occasions payment might be provided without any reminders or instructions given which in the language of service science might argue for treating the payment as a separate encounter. Likewise, an encounter that occurs rarely or perhaps only once, such as with a guide at a tourist attraction, differs from encounters occurring repeatedly for instance between a teacher and student. The questions for us are what do we gain by describing services as comprised of service encounters and what is lost if we fail to acknowledge their complexity, ambiguity, and variability?

It is also important to reflect on why some encounters and touch point interactions are called out as constituents of a service while others go unnoticed and with what consequences? A child sitting in a classroom watching other children answer a teacher's questions may easily get left out of descriptions of the student-teacher service encounters.. But the lack of an overt exchange does not mean that this student is not engaged in the educational service for better or worse.

Similarly, service encounters are perspectival and depend on individuals' relationships to the service being provided. For example, what McDonald's views as service encounters within the context of their fast food service may differ from the views of the patrons of the restaurant. Diners may include the interactions they have with others at the restaurant as a vital aspect of the service delivered by McDonald's (Glusko, 2010). Service providers are focusing more on these non-transactional aspects of the experiences of their customers (Pine and Gilmore, 1998, 1999) requiring an assessment of what is missed by taking too narrow a view of service encounter. Clearly, it is overly restrictive to label as service encounters only those interactions that involve the exchange of money (the ordering of food or payment) or that imply a formal institutional relationship (between fast food employee and customer). As we saw in Chapter 3 in our discussion of the shifts in the services performed in and by families, services involve encounters where no monetary exchange is involved. Once the requirement of a financial or institutional transaction is relaxed, social interactions occurring in a myriad of different contexts arguably can be thought of as service encounters. For example, when a friend gives a ride to the airport or a family experiencing a loss is comforted by neighbors, a service is rendered. This quickly can expand to viewing all interactions as service encounters.

Even if we restrict ourselves to what might be called "formal" service encounters, we still must consider how the interests of those who describe or design the service influence what is called out as a service encounter. For example, the interaction an elderly woman has with her daughter before using an ATM to withdraw money from her bank may not be thought of as a service encounter from the bank's perspective. And yet this interaction may be consequential in defining the banking service from the perspective of the bank customer. From the point of view of the elderly woman, the interaction with her daughter may be a fundamental part of the ATM banking service. Failure to include interactions among family members such as this one might limit how the bank defines new possibilities to enhance the banking service. Likewise, waiting in a queue in a doctor's office can be viewed as an inconvenience to be lessened by the availability of out-of-date magazines or daytime TV, or viewed as an opportunity for the clinic to provide information about health and wellness services. An anthropology of services asks us to consider interaction that seem to fall outside narrow descriptions of a service as they may point to unforeseen opportunities to assess and (re)design the service.

These examples point to another potential limitation to the concept of service encounter as it is frequently described. There is often an assumption that an individual actor is interacting with "the service," overlooking the important role of *social* context in shaping the encounter and defining possibilities for action and interaction. People come to service encounters with expectations that are learned throughout their lives. For example, some of the failures in providing quality healthcare services stem from a lack of understanding of recipients' social, cultural, and material context, including the role that other family members and the larger community play in health related-activities (Saha et al., 2008). King et al. (2007) show how managing and treating coronary artery disease for First Nation people in the Americas is influenced by the relationship patients have with their ethnic community, in addition to individual socio-demographic characteristics and existing material conditions such as transportation and housing. An anthropology of services would guide us to extend the service encounter concept beyond a narrow focus on individual interactions with a service provider to include consideration of people's practices—what it means to participate in and be part of a particular social milieu (see Meroni and Sangiorgi, 2011 for a similar argument).

Service encounters also must be located within frames that members of a society understand and value, because they implicate "matters of concern" (Latour, 2004, 2005) and the practical ways through which knowledge is produced through everyday activities. This means that there is work involved in educating people to recognize and value service encounters, and this work is performed in specific social contexts which again returns us to broader practices in societies. Indeed, as Hanser (2008) argues in her ethnographic account of retail service in a Chinese department store, service encounters play an important role in forming and reproducing social hierarchies. To isolate service encounters analytically is perilous as we may miss the broader place they have in society. Likewise, Oakes (1990) conceptualizes sales encounters in the life insurance industry as "moral arenas" in which personal identities are forged, a theme also explored by Leidner (1993). Describing the triad of company, agent, and customer Leidner (1993: 87) states, "Agents' routines are designed not simply to limit their decision-making scope but also to enhance their power, vis-à-vis prospective customers, and hence over the many aspects of their selves, including their emotions, values, and ways of thinking."

Similarly, in juxtaposition to our discussion of how traditional family labor, such as meal preparation, increasingly is being performed by strangers, today many service workers with no ongoing personal relationship to their customers or clients are called upon to demonstrate concern for their well-being. This type of work has been referred to as emotional labor where empathizing with strangers is one of the defining characteristics (Hochschild, 1983; Macdonald and Sirianni, 1996). Workers must mask their "true" feelings to present a positive and supportive demeanour to their clients and customers often adding to the stress of the job (Steinberg and Figart, 1999). Service encounters cannot be understood apart from their role in shaping individuals and reproducing values and distinctions among categories of people, as well as defining agency.

Service encounters are often presented in the service science literature as neutral, familiar and natural, but in fact they are quite complex and nuanced, and laden with significance. The concept of service encounter makes services identifiable—made up of encounters—and yet these interactions have a deeper and more integrated place in people's lives. "Seeing" encounters as constitutive of services may make sense to service scientists, but to the customers, clients, or service recipients those encounters may not be so separate or distinct from the other interactions they have day-in and day-out.

4.3   SERVICE SYSTEMS

Services have been characterized as best understood as part of service systems where people, technology, and internal and external service systems are connected via value propositions and shared information (Spohrer and Maglio, 2010). The concept of service system is inclusive, starting with a single person as the smallest service system and extending to the world economy as the largest (Maglio et al., 2009). The service system concept focuses attention on the specific connections between people and things through which value is created. A hospital providing services to patients, doctors, and staff, for example, could be described as a service system where the activities of a coordinated set of actors (entities) are needed to create value. The connection between such entities as pharmaceutical companies providing medicines, credentialing bodies certifying doctors and nurses, databases storing patient paper and digital records, hospital beds and other medical equipment, information systems scheduling procedures and visits, and so on are connected in specific ways to deliver value.

The list of entities can be very long and deciding what is within the service system and what is outside ultimately depends on the purposes for which the system is being designated. But the aim of service scientists is to identify the connections and interdependencies between the entities of the system that are required for value to be created. For example, in the case of hospital services, the value for the patients might be in lives saved and for the doctors in demonstrating their expertise and improving their skills. The value for staff might be in advancing their careers and receiving remuneration for their services, whereas for the hospitals receiving fees from insurance companies, patients, and others might define the value they receive.

Service systems often are described as existing in the world waiting to be discovered by service researchers (Alter, 2008; Basole and Rouse, 2008; Spohrer and Maglio, 2008; Vargo et al., 2008). Their reification often brings with it an assumption of a coherent, bounded entity where what is inside and outside the system is unambiguous. This reification is made clear when service systems are granted agency and described as acting in the world. For example, Vargo et al. (2008: 146) assert that, "service systems engage in exchange with other service systems to enhance adaptability and survivability, thus co-creating value for—for themselves and others." These claims lead us to reflect on the practices through which some entities become part of the service system and others are omitted. In the hospital example under what circumstances might non-traditional healers be considered part of the hospital service system or the competing services of medical tourism where patients seek less expensive option in other countries? The point is that service systems are created—they do not simply exist in the world independent of their creators. This leads us to ask how the elements of a service system are assembled, what training is needed to see them, and whether or not everyone will define particular service systems in the same way. An anthropology of services invites us to explore answers to these questions, showing how service systems are actively constructed by those who study and design them. By doing so it further acknowledges that different knowledge traditions, for example engineering or marketing or anthropology, will highlight different aspects of service systems for their own purposes.

While it may be useful to conceptualize services as providing a way to "create a seamless system of linked activities that solves customer problems" (Gustafsson and Johnson, 2003: 29), such a formulation runs the risk of overlooking the ways services are dysfunctional or create problems, and it may obscure alternative ways of conceptualizing services beyond a problem—solution framing. In this way service system discourse is open to some of the same critiques have been leveled against functionalist arguments in anthropology (Radcliffe-Brown, 1952) where the existence of some entity or activity is explained by the role it plays in preserving the system (Bubandt and Otto, 2010; Clifford and Marcus, 1986; Segal and Yanagisako, 2005). This teleological argument cannot easily explain dysfunction (Merton, 1968) and omits consideration for the possibility that certain activities are the result of historical antecedents and serve no current function.

The discourse of service systems can give a false sense of unity, inhibiting critical reflection on the ways the system as delimited may silence some voices. Moreover, by emphasizing the ability to engineer service systems to be efficient and effective as systems, entities that fall outside the boundaries of the system as defined may be more easily overlooked with unrecognized consequences. For example, our efforts to create hospital services that are more efficient and effective from the perspective of insurance companies may inadvertently leave out consideration of the needs of cultural minorities whose life-worlds fall outside the system as engineered for efficiency and marketability.

While the notion of a service system may suggests that services can be the object of scientific inquiry and can be described and engineered, it is precisely because services are open and fragmentary that our ability to specify design requirements and directly tie those requirements to desired outcomes is imperfect. This is not to claim that services are random or unstructured, only that they deviate from how formal systems operate. Services are less designed and more assembled from fragments of practices, institutions, lifestyles, technologies, and networks. As we take up in Chapter 5, this in turn suggests that the unity of control and meaning that allows designers to convert intentions into designed "products" is constrained in important ways.

4.4   CONCLUSION

We reviewed three of the central concepts of service science—services, service encounter, and service system. Those who developed these concepts did so to promote a systematic way of describing and analyzing services apart from the local knowledge and practices that grounds specific services. The concepts are useful because they promise rigorous and consistent ways of understanding and theorizing about services. They make sense to us because they are largely consistent with the world views of members of the contemporary societies in which service science has developed.

The concepts of service science often are presented in ways that suggest a neutral, outside observer looking onto service worlds. The concepts are couched in a language that is familiar to us with talk of encounters and interactions people have with each other and the material world. But a singularity of perspective can obscure the multiple and sometimes conflicting experiences of actors differently positioned within service worlds. The practices of those who define services and who suggest how they can best be acted upon—designed, improved, optimized—have consequences for how we understand service worlds. As such, they describe something much broader than services—they shape how we understand the human condition.

An anthropology of services problematizes the very concepts we use to describe service worlds, such as services, service encounter, and service system. This is not to argue that these concepts be discarded, but to make us aware of how they limit and necessarily circumscribe where and how we intervene in service worlds. Our exploration of service concepts also has given us a chance to learn about the community of practice of those who have been developing these concepts and accompanying vocabulary. What we have seen is that while the service science community may be somewhat heterogeneous, it is largely comprised of people and organizations with interests in business, marketing, management, engineering, and IT. While we do not disparage these fields, it is important to note that they have shaped the questions that are framed within the service science community. Much of the knowledge that has been generated in this growing field of inquiry is the sort of propositional knowledge that is foundational to academic scholarship. This knowledge represents a distinctive way of looking at services and inevitably raises questions about the scope of service science and its ways of analyzing services.

Service science has largely developed in post-industrial capitalist societies and we speculate that the issues and questions raised would be different if they originated from a different starting point. Our critical reflection on the concepts of services, service encounters, and service systems thrusts us back into the messiness of everyday lives. Regardless of whether we are describing a service, teasing apart the "props" of encounters, or navigating around the complex terrain of systems, we soon find ourselves looking at the practices of people participating in service worlds and of those who venture to describe and intervene in them.

CHAPTER 5

Design and its Limits

As we were becoming aware of the language and concepts used to describe services we were also hearing about efforts to design services and service systems so they could be optimized and outcomes could be controlled. Not wanting to leave service outcomes to chance, strategies and approaches were being developed to intentionally design services and manage them over time. As the service sector had become such an important part of the world economy it was understandable that people would want to explicitly create service offerings and to control their impacts. That services should be designed seemed reasonable, but the very abstractness of services as transformations and as co-produced through human interactions led us to ask in what ways the intentional design of services even made sense.

On our journey we were encountering services at a time when design had ascended as a professional field with its own specialized discourse that was being applied to an ever expanding list of domains, even including the design of interactions (Winograd, 1997; Zimmerman et al., 2007; Stolterman, 2008) and experiences (Pine and Gilmore, 1999; Buxton, 2007; Hassenzahl, 2010). Designing, it seemed, was becoming ubiquitous and no longer restricted to the design of things. It held out the promise of helping to solve a myriad of human problems (Thackara, 2005). And so we needed to look at design not merely as processes for creating goods, but more broadly as a metaphor for how we think about and effect change in the world.

Contemporary design has been presented as an activity performed by specialists following professional training. Yet, as anthropologists we understand design to be a basic human capability. The dwellings, bracelets, and canoes of the Trobriand Islanders, were made by people and so reflect their visions of beauty and usefulness. Likewise, humans were able to visualize hand axes and other tools within stones that had just the right properties and to devise methods to liberate them for use. Both the artifact and the ways of working stone reflect human intention and so both object and process can be said to be designed. For those early humans and for ourselves, designing presumes that the world is a place that can be made better by modifying it—a perfect world would have no need for design.

Despite the continuity between designing past and present, designers today can seem like wizards who see new possibilities and have abilities to realize them that exceed those of ordinary folk. At least in the popular press, design seems to promise control of outcomes, yet through the lens of a practice approach we were impelled to question both the wisdom of empowering people to so control others and the reality of being able to do so. Design discourse often presumed that designers could turn intentions into outcomes and as such specify the "user experience." In what follows we take a look at some of the ways design has been understood with the aim of deepening our understanding of its role in designing services.

5.1   DESIGN BACKGROUND AND ISSUES

Design theorist Richard Buchanan (2001: 9) claims, "Design is the human power of conceiving, planning, and making products that serve human beings in the accomplishment of their individual and collective purposes" and Herbert Simon (1981: 129) noted in *The Sciences of the Artificial* that "everyone designs who devises courses of action aimed at changing existing situations into preferred ones." Design is instrumental in bringing about "better" products and situations.

While design may be a general human capability, Buchanan points out that design assumes various "orders." Symbols and things are the focus of Buchanan's first- and second-order design and are associated with graphic and industrial design, respectively. The focus of third-order design is action, of which services are exemplary. Fourth-order design focuses on the intentional creation of environments and systems. Although "everyone designs," these orders are associated with specialized disciplines in which people receive training to be better than others at bringing form to their ideas.

Design often is characterized as enabling people to find solutions to problems. Rowe (1998) draws on the broad literature about problem solving in his discussion of architectural design. He differentiates well-defined problems from ill-defined and "wicked" ones, where well-defined or tame problems are those with prescribed ends or goals where only the means to solve them remain to be chosen. In ill-defined problems, both ends and means are unknown in their entirety at the outset, leading to a process of working back and forth between problem and solution. Wicked problems lack even the possibility of becoming fully defined and require a stop rule to terminate the design process. Solutions here may not be judged correct or incorrect since there are always plausible alternative solutions to wicked problems. These problem formulations matter, says Rowe, since the style of completed projects is largely determined by the initial design ideas introduced by the designer and the problem solving process that is used.

Archaeologist David Kingery (2001: 133) also reminds us that a distinctive but general approach to problem solving has been the most important design tool through prehistory, history, and the present. Design is largely about making tradeoffs among imperfect alternatives and not simply about producing what is imagined. Kingery goes on to suggest that it is through the extension of "normal configurations" that artifacts are made to meet the needs of different groups of producers, users, and distributors. For example, automobiles, chairs, and houses are recognizable by their normal configurations. Ways of addressing needs can be behavioral as well as technological, so dining in a restaurant or negotiating with a mechanic is a normal configuration that can be improved through design. The normal configuration allows us to recognize objects, machines, and systems from the prehistoric past to the present, and it provides a basis for evaluating new designs. It shifts attention from individuals to collectivities, from individual cognition (the lone designer) to actions in the world, and to evidence that can be inspected and discussed.

Humans have expectations for the purposes, functions, and performances of normally configured entities. Paper plates, for example, appear to be simple, but they are accompanied by expectations. They should be more rigid than a sheet of paper, have a three-dimensional profile, and last through a meal, but also be decomposable. They should be inexpensive so they can be discarded and typically should hold-up for only one meal so there is no expectation they will survive a thorough scrubbing. Expectations of performance precede design and our creations are judged against them. Through designing we may discover that our performance expectations of the object are unrealistic and we need to revise them. People make assessments about assigning failure or achievement, and results are measured against socially-constructed standards of normal expectation.

Kingery's discussion suggests a broad view of how we conceptualize designing and how it is connected to social life. Designing can be found across artifacts, services, policies, and spaces, and even in working relationships. He argues that although it rests upon a foundation of problem solving, it is so much more than linking problems and solutions, with the accompanying sense of finality and closure. To the contrary, as Gunn and Donovan (2012b: 1) argue, "a process of design thus is not to impose closure but to allow for everyday life to carry on." Design, in this view, is more ambiguous, diffuse, and embedded in the ordinary than assumed in many definitions of design that equate it with the exercise of expertise to shape outcomes and, ultimately, the behavior of users. Instead of attending to passive consumers whose needs are met by active designers, we are thrust into a world of skilled practitioners who appropriate a myriad of (designed) objects into their lives. An implication is that the objects of design are never really finished as their incorporation into practices is ongoing.

Descriptions of design almost always assume an ability of humans to exert control or power in the world in order to shape it to match their vision. Things are designed to have specific characteristics and the designer's ability is demonstrated by the ability to produce them. But there are complex linkages between ideas, representations on paper or screens, the artifacts that emerge, and the performances that bring them to life. There is a chain of reasoning and much of it is tacit, with many assumptions made along the way. Designers do not design in totality the outcomes they want because they can never fully specify how their designs will be taken up by people. Given this, some have suggested that what designers can do is design "potentials"—the conditions that they believe can make a result more or less likely. Nelson and Stolterman (2003: 2) note that, "The world has proven to be unpredictable, despite the best attempts of science and technology to bring predictability and control to worldly affairs." But they argue the "instrumentality of design" provides for the possibility that conditions can be created that render some outcomes more likely than others and thus enable humans to drive change in desired directions. Likewise, Wahl and Baxter (2008: 73) voice optimism for design by remarking, "… rather than believing that we can design universally applicable blueprints to bring about sustainability by prediction and control-based, top-down engineering, it may be more useful and appropriate to think of the outcome(s) as an emergent property of the complex dynamic system in which we all participate, co-create, and adapt to interdependent biophysical and psycho-social processes."

While these authors understand that humans do not completely control outcomes through their design intentions, they argue that by conceptualizing the world as a complex, dynamic system the negative consequences of our designs can perhaps be limited. But even more, they draw attention to the importance of designers having a "theory" of the world and its people. Designers do not simply design in and for the world in general but for particular conceptualizations of it. These in turn shape ideas about problems and solutions, causes and effects, and assumptions and values. In this sense, designers create the worlds for which they design.

5.2   DESIGN PROCESS AND KNOWLEDGE

Design is a process that unfolds in specific ways through time. It involves inquiry, with an eye to synthesis and ultimately to creating. Operating within constraints is the *sine qua non* of designing whether in the context of a needs assessment, problem formulation, or the exigencies of everyday life. Design processes enable the designer to create within those constraints.

Zeisel (2006) describes a design process that consists of three elementary activities of imaging, presenting, and testing. *Imaging* is the ability to go beyond any information given to see or create something—a building or artifact or service—where nothing now exists. Going beyond what is given, looking for what is missing is a hallmark of designing (Cross, 2007: 24-25). *Presenting* consists of the ways that designers externalize their images, and while sketches, models, and photographs are common design artifacts, textual descriptions also enable the externalization of ideas that allows both communication and reflection to support further imaging. *Testing* involves comparing the design against designers' and clients' implicit expectation, the problem constraints or solution objectives, notions of internal consistency, and performance criteria. Testing transforms the design process from one of blind search to the formulation of alternatives and specific ways choices are made among them.

Zeisel (2006) further notes that design unfolds through time with changing visions of the final product. Initial images are refined and modified in a process marked by creative leaps triggered by testing that makes apparent contradictions and inconsistencies in the specific design. Design moves toward a range of acceptable responses, rather than a single optimal solution. Criteria for acceptability can change as the problem formulation and solutions develop, but designs are generally assessed against how they perform in specific environments and how the elements of the design are internally consistent.

The episodic organization of design is also noted by Rowe (1998) who explains that episodes in the design process are defined by "skirmishes" with facets of the problem. The episodes cohere and provide direction, albeit not as a simple linear progression. Instead, episodes are characterized by to and fro movement between areas of concern. There are periods of speculation followed by frenetic, churning ideation, and then assessment of what has been proposed. Calmer periods of taking stock and reassessing strategies follow, with the episodes of design having their own distinctive rhythms. Each episode has an orientation, an organizing principle that takes on a life of its own that can include pressing ahead if only to see what happens—followed by back tracking to clarify, assess, and revise. As the scope of the problem becomes narrowed and finite, the episodes become less distinct. For Zeisel (2006), this means that design is best envisioned as a spiraling process that includes backtracking and leaping ahead, repetition with shifting foci, and defining a zone of acceptable responses that, when entered, permits a decision to be made to build or implement. Designing takes time and while often presented as a unified process, episodes of designing are neither linear nor uniform. Tension and inconsistency are not threats to be eliminated, but provide the dynamics that pushes the design ahead, albeit often in fits and starts.

5.3   REPRESENTING AND BUILDING

As Kingery (2001) observes, there was a time when those who imagined artifacts were also their makers as well as their users. For much of human history, and for many parts of contemporary everyday life, things are made without benefit of scientific or theoretical understandings. Lawson (2006) uses George Sturt's classic account of making a wooden cart wheel in a 19th century wheelwright's shop to illustrate the point. Such wheels were fabricated in ways that seemed counterintuitive or inexplicable, but which were necessary for the wheel to properly function. These wheels were not built from blueprints, but from the craft knowledge of woodworkers, leaving scholars uncertain about the reasons for the specific characteristics of the 19th century wheels described by Sturt.

Designers today typically do not implement or build what they design. Christopher Alexander (1964) describes the shift to a self-conscious design process driven by a cultural shift to working in new settings or contexts, and with new technologies, materials, and purposes. This he argues can isolate the designer from the artifact produced and has led to "design by drawing" where the drawings are part of the thinking process and not just for communication. They permit rapid investigation and experimentation, although drawings are limited in what they can convey and how that information can be manipulated. "The modern designer then experiments not with the object itself but with representations of it" (Lawson, 2004: 32). Drawings are so important in design because they are more than representations of things in the world; they are extensions of thinking throughout the design process.

With Lawson (2004) as our guide, we can explore a few drawings types and their uses. *Presentation drawings* convey the final look of an artifact in order to communicate with a client making the decision to proceed or not. They are intelligible and compelling to novices and do not require specialized expertise to understand. Compare this to *instruction drawings* that are used for physically creating the object, requiring expertise to be read. Diagrams in the form of charts and graphs help designers visualize functional relations. They can dematerialize form and highlight functional relationships, such as a subway map that is useful but not as a representation of the spatial layout of the city. Diagrams remove information thereby allowing designers to focus on some features, but not all. *Proposition drawings* allow designers to propose alternatives in which features of the design are externalized in order to examine them. These drawings remind us that designing is more than a process of adding details. They are central to design because they temporarily freeze a feature so we can stand back and consider the implications. By enabling designers to explore particular features, proposition drawings enable designers to engage in conversations with the drawing thus provoking responses in the overall design, and vice versa.

The types of drawings we have discussed come from architecture and industrial design, where material objects are being created, but they nonetheless can inform our understanding of the more abstract endeavor of service design. They provide tangible evidence of the back and forth movement within the design process. Drawings do not march lockstep from general representations rendered in broad brushstrokes to precise blueprints of specific elements. Different types of drawing punctuate the process and reinforce the idea that the design process is far from a linear one proceeding directly from idea to realization. As Lawson reminds us, there is constant risk that designers will grant authority to the drawing by confusing the rendering with the realized artifact. Perspective and scale can easily be massaged so that even the impossible seems realistic, but of course ultimately drawings of physical artifacts can be assessed against their material form. Such tests are difficult in service design since what is being rendered is more diffuse and involves many more elements that are outside the designers control or even imagination.

Drawing inevitably creates bounded wholes by distinguishing and depicting some things and not others. The creation of wholes is well illustrated by renderings of archaeological sites. The drawing freezes time so "every architectural feature exists at the same time on the surface of the page" (McFadyen 2012: 107). What is described may have been built over millennia, just as other elements may have been destroyed. But the drawing depicts it as a whole in which we encounter "preconceived ideas materialized into forms" (McFadyen 2012: 108). The drawing creates a whole and locates the creative impulse in the idea as represented, rather than in its use.

This bounding performed through representation also demarcates a start and ending, and so it reinforces design as a discrete activity. This may not be problematic in the design of objects, but it is when we consider services that involve human interactions and relationships that predate and extend beyond the designated design phases. Such implied temporal bounding perhaps unintentionally divides the world between periods of design and non-design, between creation and use, and between services as depicted and as enacted.

Ultimately, drawings do not build; people do. Drawings, including blueprints, are taken by people who do something with them. In fact, this process of building may be a more helpful metaphor for the how services come to be rather than design since it draws our attention to how things are made through acting in the world. Davis (1999: 15) introduces the concept of "cultures of building" or "the coordinated system of knowledge, procedures, and habits that surrounds the building process in a given place and time." A culture of building not only facilitates construction but it connects the building to a larger social context. That process of building is complex and includes steps of deciding to build, choosing and selecting appropriate sites, regulating the character and placement of building on these sites, financing the construction, designing the building, producing and supplying materials, constructing the building, regulating or managing the construction, and occupying, using, and modifying the building.

Design is only one step in the process and that process itself is largely initiated and controlled by institutions where building is understood not as an isolated act but as part of complex social processes. Because different institutions have different agendas, a building is created not simply through consensus about the final product, but by bringing together actors who perform in accordance with their own practices. They may have little in common with one another and operate relatively independently, and while their agendas are individually comprehensible there can be controversy and inconsistency in how these different actors relate to that which is being built.

The metaphor of building is suggestive of what it means to design services. Despite the intentions of designers to produce elegant, idealized services, in fact they are made real by people with their own purposes and practices. The implications are that services cannot be thought of as taken-for-granted, self-contained wholes, or as having unambiguous starting and finishing points. They are 'constructed' over time.

5.4   DESIGNING OR INTERVENING

When designers enter the scene the world is already filled with the results of human actions and intentions. Schiffer (2010) and Kingery (2001) are archaeologists whose work is relevant to how we consider design in today's world. Since that world is full of artifacts, designing from scratch is not an apt metaphor for how things get made; instead, existing resources are colonized or rearranged. Intervening in flows of ongoing activities better captures the variety of ways services come into being. This broader view of interventions implies a world of active agents who take artifacts, ideas, and social interactions and incorporate them into new arrangements that require people to enact and perpetuate them.

The connections between intention and realization are often distributed and entangled, and they are rarely compartmentalized as projects with clear starts and finishes. The path from design to production and consumption is complex and strewn with unintended consequences, and designing services is no exception. Precisely because services are embedded in cultural practices it is even more problematic to clearly bound the activities of service design. A practice approach accordingly suggests the value of recognizing that we live in a world of human productions and that we too are embedded in such practices. This forces us to ask what activities count as designing for different communities. What are the relationships between the individuals designing and the ultimate products or outcomes, if indeed either is ever ultimate? How do ideas move through disparate practices and how do they mobilize people to act in particular ways? Our practice approach sensitizes us to designing not just for people as discrete individual users, but for the practices through which things get done in the world. The shift is subtle, but significant. We speak of individuals using objects, while the performance of practices implicates material things—including people.

Designers always intervene in practices that are both stable (personally or socially) and that provide the fields in which agency is exercised. A practice approach emphasizes that designing is about interjecting something new or different into the mix, and recognizes that designers do not control how it will be used or how it will change outcomes. Design here entails creativity, including the capacity to reach out and bring artifacts, places, people and ideas together to create new assemblages. Designing becomes less a single activity or process than a string of activities which bear only a loose family resemblance to one another and which are likely to vary case by case. Design becomes a bundle of activities—"designing"—where clear starting points and static blueprints or plans give way to experimenting, reassessing, and adjusting as artifact emerges or service is enacted.

The language of design may provide a neutral, rather technocratic-speak, but design is intended to effect change and constrain what people do and so is always a matter of control and power which is shaped by the politics of the day. Much of the writing about design is about making a better world, often fostered by increased participation. But design can also be pernicious, where the design process and goals are ones we loathe and involve overt or subtle forms of control. It is risky to assume that designers are always on the side of truth, beauty and justice, and important to acknowledge that designers cannot completely control what they have unleashed. No matter how well we think we understand the practices of a community, it is dangerous to assume that the objects of our designing can simply be inserted in those practices. This also heightens the importance of reflecting on our own practices of designing. In this sense design is both less than we might have originally thought (because it is not definitive of outcomes) and more (because of the variety of activities and institutions it potentially implicates).

5.5 CONCLUSION

Designing is both a general human ability and a specialized discipline. By mastering the latter designers differentiate themselves as experts from other people. This prompts us to ask about that expertise. If design methods and techniques are not examined for what they can and cannot provide and for the expertise they claim, there is the possibility of denigrating, ignoring, or minimizing local experience or non-professional modalities for justifying action. There is a chain of reasoning from idea to action, but much of it is implicit and unspoken with important assumptions being made along the way. This means that there is work, sometimes simple and direct and other times not, in translating potentials into actions.

The object of design does not flow lineally or directly from our understanding of the situation and the desire to make it better. From the information and assumptions that construct a problem as one that is amenable to design leaps are to the design made that purportedly solves the problem as defined. While laudably design often has the goal of making things better, there is often less attention to assessing who benefits, how things are becoming better, and what are the costs now and in the future. Design efforts reflect assumptions that delimit the particular problem—solution framing which in turn determines if the beneficial intended outcomes outweigh unintended negative consequences. A practice approach requires that we examine these questions and by so doing ground designing in the broader social and historical context.

CHAPTER 6

Service Design

Our interest in the genesis of services inevitably took us to the emerging field of service design. Services, it seemed obvious, were designed through processes that were strikingly similar to what we had encountered in the broader field of design. Design was the lingua franca shared by those who were in the business of bringing services about. We were at once comforted that there was a common language designating a coherent field with familiar activities, and yet we wondered if the taken for granted language of design concealed diverse meanings and usages. The very diversity of service design practitioners suggested that the foundational knowledge of this new field of 'service design' might be masking important differences.

Service design, we soon learned, was thought by many to be the missing ingredient needed to speed service innovation (Ostrom et al., 2010) and to facilitate the integration of expertise from different disciplines, including interaction design, marketing, and technology development (Dubberly and Evenson, 2010; Kimbell, 2009, 2011; Ostrom et al., 2010; Polaine et al., 2013; Stickdorn and Schneider, 2010). Service design was on the agenda of many organizations where "a multitude of tools, many from the social sciences, are brought to bear on problems, *all under the banner of design* as an organizing principle and leitmotif" (Saco and Gonsalves, 2008: 10–11 italics added).

The focus on service design was promoting the professionalization of services, with many design firms and agencies transforming themselves into service design firms, just as new startups were entering the field. In 2004 the Service Design Network was founded with the aim of developing and establishing "the discipline and professional identity of service design" (http://www.service-design-network.org/purpose/#sthash.vPmF5BjI.dpuf) and in 2008 the first Service Design and Innovation Conference (ServDes) was held which brought together an international group of academics and practitioners interested in promoting and disseminating original research on services and service design. Paradoxically, this professionalization of service design as a distinct community of practice suggested clarity about services , the "object" of design, that we had seen was lacking. The more we understood services as embedded in society, the more we questioned assumptions about intention and wholeness as signatures of service innovation regardless of the increasingly persuasive claims about methods for their design. Indeed, we had come to question the unitary view of services and instead were asking how some social interactions, transactions, and transformations came to be identified as services while others did not.

As we witnessed the emergence of these communities of designers, researchers, and practitioners we wondered what practices were subsumed under the service design banner and how were they affecting the ability to reshape service worlds. By asking how services came to be we sought to look at the variety of activities that were included under the labels of "design" and "designing." The language of design seemed to bind together the activities of diverse fields and disciplines whose members might not even recognize each other as engaged in the common endeavor of bringing about services.

At times it seemed service design was as much about producing a coherent narrative about an emerging community of practice and defining it as a profession that controlled certain knowledge as it was about actually producing services. Much of this discourse, as in other fields, was focused on mobilizing support within and on behalf of that community in order to obtain resources, with uncertain connections to the actual work of bringing about services. The discourse of design from this perspective is concerned with securing the commitments of potential customers and enterprises to develop services. As Mosse (2005) argues in the context of international development projects, the language used to secure commitments may necessarily be quite different from that used to actually create plans for action—those plans are likely produced after resources are committed. Accordingly, we became interested not just in the discourse of service design, but also in how it was used by practitioners to achieve their own objectives.

We approached service design to get an insider's view of how services came to be, with particular interest in the narratives generated by communities of practice that described ideas moving to instantiations with all the claims for expertise and know-how required to do so. While arguments were being made that intentional acts of design could make services more "productive and satisfying" (Saco and Gonsalves, 2008: 13) and create more sustainable economies (Thackara, 2005), we suspected that the reality behind the rhetoric was far more complex than first imagined. Two questions thus came to characterize our journey through the terrain of service design. First, what are the activities that are presumed to bring about services and in what ways do they constitute "design"? Second, what is the relationship of the discourse of design and designing to the actual genesis of services and to the service design community of practice?

6.1   TWO POLES OF SERVICE DESIGN

We came to understand service design as it was shaped by two "poles" that orient services by their relationship to basic values in society. These poles exert their force in the development of any service, although their relative emphasis varies with consequences for the process of designing and for the subsequent services that emerge. In the first or the "business benefit pole," value is based on the proposition that services can entice consumers and thereby be sustained through the patronage of their users. The design challenge is typically one of formulating propositions that somehow correspond to user values and to define payment in a way that sustains the service. Central here is that the service is embedded in a business enterprise and is supported by its users, quite apart from the larger impact it might have on society for better or worse.

The second pole, which we refer to as the "societal benefit pole," is comprised of social values that orient the service independent from the "value proposition" that entices people to use the service. In fact, the benefit from the service may be distributed far beyond its immediate use, again because it is explicitly intended to enact societal values that all or some members of society embrace. The challenge is to support something that is by some measures beneficial to society, but that may not be embraced by its users at levels that guarantee sustainability.

We conceptualize the business and societal benefits as poles because they exist in a tension with each other, although they are not mutually exclusive. Each raises different questions and makes different assumptions about people, organizations, values, and society. They also draw on different practices that reflect assumptions about people, sociotechnical arrangements, organizations, and technology, just as service design "incorporates elements and tools from several domains to attain various and, at times, competing objectives: customer satisfaction or appreciation, designer satisfaction or sense of accomplishment, problem resolution, economic and environmental sustainability, and practical beauty (beauty that works)" (Saco and Gonsalves, 2008: 12).

From the perspective of the business pole, service design often is viewed as a way to increase business performance in the service sector (Maffei, et al., 2005). In a recent report of the European Commission on Design for Innovation (Dervojeda et. al., 2014: 5) the authors point to "the transformative power of service design which is understood as the process through which services disrupt traditional channels to market, business processes and models, to significantly enhance customer experience in a way that impacts upon the value chain as a whole." An effectively managed service then "should function seamlessly for customers to perceive it correctly (as designed)" (Goldstein et al., 2002: 122), with a unity of purpose to create "integrated, memorable, and favorable customer experience" (Bitner et al., 2008: 69).

Framed in the context of business benefit, participants are seen as owners, managers, and customers of services, with pressure to consider service productivity and efficiency as critical measures of business success. However, increasingservice productivity is difficult since many of the assumptions that underlie productivity models for manufacturing are absent for services (Grönroos and Ojasalo, 2004). For example, changes in how a service is delivered can affect the quality of the output either directly or in the perception of clients. This renders one of the key ways to increase productivity in manufacturing through changes in input resources less reliable for services (Gadrey and Gallouj, 2002). Consequently, fewer workers or less time to perform the service may degrade the service at the same time it increases productivity. Service quality, and therefore value for clients, ise effected for many services by a reduction in input resources. As a result, service design frequently has targeted measures of service performance, rather than productivity, as essential to their success.

However, complicating the ability to measure service performance is the observation noted earlier that "value is embedded in the experiences co-created by the individual in an experience environment that the company co-develops with consumers" (Prahalad and Ramaswamy, 2004: 121).

As such, designers are constrained in the control they have over service performance. Furthermore, too narrow a concern with the "value" a recipient of the service receives discounts larger societal consequences such as sustainability or community wellbeing. Consequently, viewing service design as a means to improve performance in an effort to maintain or increase service "consumption" favors innovations that deliver business success sometimes at the expense of societal benefit.

In contrast to valuing service design as key to business benefit and economic success, service design can also be framed as a means of enabling human betterment and sustainability—indeed, it has been seen by some as a way to bring about a more just and sustainable world (Thackara, 2005; Vezzoli and Manzini, 2008). Services, it is argued, can be a force for social good by helping to address the myriad of problems the world is facing. Singleton (2009: 9) further champions the instrumentality of service to "shape the possibilities open to individuals and groups, creating the platforms on which practices of everyday life might take hold and flourish or be slowly extinguished." Arguing that the world we live in didn't just happen but is the result of "design" choices made by urban planners, legislators, bankers and a myriad of others, Thackara (2005: 6) suggests that by better understanding how the world came to be as it is, "we can better describe where we want to be. With alternative situations evocatively in mind, we can design our way from here to there. Through acts of design it is possible to create more livable and sustainable worlds."

As laudable as these aspirations are they rest on assumptions about the meaning of social good and the ability to turn design ideas into expected outcomes. In this sense services depend on knowledge of human actions, motivations, meanings and values to further problem solving for social good. A practice approach to designing services necessitates that service designers see themselves as unavoidably part of "networks of working relations" through which services are designed, implemented and enacted. In this sense attention is directed toward the connections between actions and outcomes, and the located accountabilities or "multiple, located, partial perspectives that find their objective character through ongoing processes of debate" (Suchman, 2002: 92).

Where service design is situated in relation to the business and societal benefit poles has implications for how people are involved in service design. Related to the idea that services can foster human betterment is the notion of "user" participation in design, where the motive for participation is both instrumental and political (Simonsen and Roberson, 2012). Participation is instrumental in the sense that design outcomes will be improved or better suited to the needs of users if the latter are involved in their design and political in the sense that participation seeks to empower those whose lives are affected by new innovations in their design. While participatory design has its roots in Scandinavian worker rights legislation (Clement and Van den Besselaar, 1993; Kensing and Blomberg, 1998; Schuler and Namioka, 1993), it has been embraced as a useful strategy in the design of everything from soap to social services, often without the political commitment of empowerment that motivated its early proponents.. Indeed, participation in design transcends the business- and societal-benefit poles, although they influence the roles given to people in designing services, as consumers or partners.

Saco and Goncalves (2008: 13) further argue that involving people in service design is especially relevant as they are "already involved in production and delivery," this in contrast to product design. In a related way Blomberg (2009) argues that participatory design is relevant to service design beyond as a strategy for designing. By treating potential users as partners, she suggests that the principles of participatory design (Greenbaum and Kyng, 1991; Kensing and Blomberg, 1998) can be usefully thought of as potential design elements in new service offerings. As such, she argues that services might benefit from according service recipients and providers *access to each other's domains of knowledge* and supporting the *joint negotiation of* service *outcomes*—both principles of participatory design.

Service designers have taken on the banner of participation arguing that citizens, patients, students, and other service recipients should be co-designers in the services of governments, hospitals, and educational institutions alike. Meroni and Sangiorgi (2011: 14) argue that "what is different from traditional participatory approaches is the addition of the 'co-creation' concept where users are now looked at as the biggest untapped resources in the public service delivery system." So "users" are not only co-designers, but through their engagement in enacting the service they are also continuously co-producers of it. Some commentators further argue that broadening user involvement in design and innovation provides for the common good independent of any specific business benefit (Von Hippel, 2009; Lessig, 2005).

However, there is a risk that user or customer participation becomes cooptation where customers' ongoing involvement in design (as co-producers of service outcomes) ensnares and implicates them in the agendas of service providers which may not be in their best interest (Thrift, 2006). The possibilities for such cooptation has become even more pronounced as more and more service providers are mining the activities of their users as they co-produce the service. For example, Google searches and Facebook posts are used to target ads to the users of their service. These firms prototype new services to enlist their customers in the development of new services so "more and more design activity is not defined in relation to a final endpoint. Rather, the "production process has no final goals, no natural target or final user, but rather continuously feeds on itself" (Thrift, 2006: 295). Thought of in this way, services are being designed for user or customer involvement, often without their knowledge or consent, with the assumption of the value and inevitability of an ever changing set of outcomes or transformations.

6.2   OBJECTS OF SERVICE DESIGN

As we engaged with the service design community in various venues (Blomberg and Evenson, 2006; Emergence Conference, 2006; Sangiorgi et al., 2014) we came to appreciate one of the central puzzles of these communities—what are the objects of service design? Our exploration led us to question how transformations brought about by services were linked to the conditions that brought them about, for it seemed there was an assumed logical link between conditions and transformations. We also wondered about the possibility of "hidden" practices that were not made visible in the identification of the desired or intended transformations. We speculated that these practices might be lost in abstractions of the service necessary and inevitable in the design process and as such were invisible (Star, 1991a, 1991b) or relegated to the role of presumed or uninteresting background.

As we learned in Chapter 4, a common definition of services is the application of human or mechanical effort to bring about changes or transformations in people or objects. This suggests a legitimate focus for service design might be on the outcomes or transformations brought about through such efforts (Kimbell, 2011). In addition, because services are viewed as more than their material embodiment, and involve the performances of both providers and recipients as they enact the service, performances also represent a reasonable object of service design (Secomandi and Snelders, 2011). Likewise, "touch points" and "service encounters" offer possible foci for design since they represent the times when service providers and recipients interact, either directly or mediated by technology, to "produce" or "co-create" service (Clatworthy, 2011). While there are many ways to conceptualize the objects of service design, the choices made have implications for the practices of service design, including the know-how of the actors involved. We explore some of these implications.

Focusing on designing for outcomes—the transformations that designers would like to achieve—suggests a strategy of working backwards from outcomes to consider the various levers or resources available to help realize outcomes. Service design's object then is to specify the conditions or prerequisites required to make service transformations possible (Secomandi and Snelders, 2011: 23-24). It is not the enacted service that is being designed, but instead the conditions necessary to achieve particular outcomes. In this sense service design shares many characteristics with interaction and experience design with their focus on the sociotechnical affordances that enable interactions and define experiences (Holmlid, 2007; Patrício et al., 2008; Zomerdijk and Voss, 2010). For example, Starbucks creates the conditions—comfortable chairs, engaging music, access to Wi-Fi, and of course coffee and tea drinks made to the customer's liking—that deliver an experience unlike those possible in 1950s coffee shops or the McDonald's of today. Similarly, an educational service aiming to create better informed students might focus on designing textbooks, the physical layout of the classroom, teaching methodologies, and so on—the prerequisites—that increase the likelihood of students learning the specific course content.

However, it is not easy to know where to draw the line concerning what to include as prerequisite for achieving particular service outcomes. In some sense the entirety of the sociomaterial world in which services are enacted is "prerequisite" for whatever outcomes are achieved. For example, access to transportation may be a prerequisite to obtaining healthcare services, or digital literacy may be a prerequisite for benefiting from online college courses. In this sense the design of healthcare services involves the design of transportation systems and the design MOOCs (massive open online courses) includes the design of curriculum to foster digital literacy. Arguably these prerequisites would be needed to deliver health outcomes and to ensure that the benefits of online courses reach all those in need. That said, outcomes too are complex social constructs that include tangible or intangible consequences, as well as temporary or lasting benefits making the choice of which prerequisites to design for that much more challenging.

Consideration of the prerequisites needed to realize particular outcomes broadens the scope of design to include such things as governmental policies that support or compel the provision of certain services; business models that connect ecosystem partners, define revenue streams, and delineate recipient groups; sociotechnical infrastructures upon which services are delivered; technologies that enable service relationships; and physical spaces in which services are enacted. Each design focus in turn brings certain actors to the fore and requires different strategies for connecting what is inside and what is outside any particular design effort (Blomberg and Kimbell, 2014). In this sense service design is implicated in the disciplinary projects of engineering, marketing, business, governmental policy, and architecture; each with their own interests and particular ways of intervening in service worlds.

We might usefully broaden the question to include where and when to intervene in service worlds to make some transformations more likely and others less so. Arguing for "accepting the fundamental inability of design to completely plan and regulate services" Meroni and Sangiorgi (2011: 10) suggest instead that designers create "the right conditions for certain forms of interactions and relationships to happen." In this sense service design rests upon theories of human behavior, how people will be inclined to act, the practices and know-how that condition what is reasonable or even possible. As Thackara (2005: 7) observes, "designers are having to evolve from being the individual authors of objects, or buildings, to being the facilitators of change among large groups of people." The argument is that without presupposing that designers can control how people interact with each other or their surroundings, they can create certain conditions that will make some interactions and encounters more likely than others. The challenge of service design is to reduce the gap between what the designer imagines and the world as experienced, given all the intermediaries and historical antecedents that shape futures.

Broadening the scope of service design may seem to complicate and unreasonably expand the designer's role beyond areas in which she is comfortable or feels empowered. Furthermore, the expectation that any one designer or design project will be able to address in any meaningful way the myriad of potential influences on service outcomes is likely unreasonable. Designers may be highly expert in some domains of knowledge but not others. Service design effectively requires that designers connect to different kinds of knowledge and know-how with varying degrees of attainment. For example, there is theoretical knowledge about technology or business processes, practice-based knowledge of local activities, and skill-based knowledge of service blueprinting. Not every designer can be expected to navigate these domains equally. That said, the multiple and varied sites for service design offer many potential opportunities to shape outcomes, each requiring different sets of skills and implicating the designer and design project in particular accountabilities to actors and outcomes.

6.3   ACTIVITIES OF SERVICE DESIGN

The unified language of service design combined with the sheer variety of activities that fall under this both suggests a richness to the field and at the same time risks portraying it as more homogenous than it is. While there has been a proliferation of service design methodologies, many include a set of recognizable steps borrowed from product design. Dubberly and Evenson (2010) present service design as a familiar, elegant sequence of activities (see Figure 6.1). The first step of *observation* involves a description of the environment and "user and stakeholder needs identification." The next step, *reflection*, includes describing the current service system and the imagined one using techniques of blueprinting and customer journey maps. The making step follows where the particular features or "resources" are designed, including the processes, enactments and "experience strategy." The next step of *socializing* creates "the network for uptake"—both within the service organization and with the customers. Finally, *implementation* occurs when system resources are "brought to life" through beta tests and fine tuning over time. By engaging in these steps designers explore possibilities, generate alternatives, and evaluate outcomes—the long-established rubric of design.

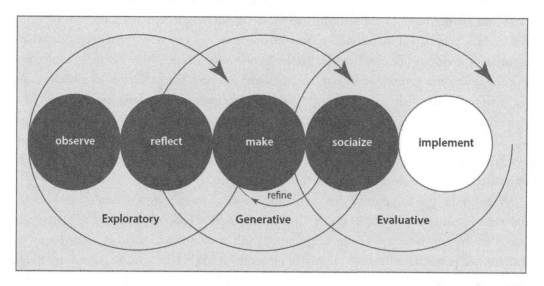

Figure 6.1: Design process. Adapted from Dubberly and Evenson (2010: 409).

While Dubberly and Evenson's design process presents service design as a familiar process, many of the concerns raised in Chapter 4 about services and service systems—that service systems are discoverable through observation and reflection, that it is possible to clearly define the boundaries of service systems, and that differently positioned actors will see and define the system differently—are not explicitly addressed. While design must fix its object if only momentarily in order to move through the steps in a design process, imagining how things might be different by making and refining, and acting upon the object by implementing and socializing, presupposes choices, often implicit, about what's inside and outside the service system. A practice approach to designing services compels us to reflect on these choices and their consequences. Furthermore, accepting these as canonical steps of service design still does not directly specify the activities of service designers as they depend on other factors such as the scope of design and where the designer is situated in relation to the overall project. In each instance different activities and sets of skills and know-how are required.

In an efffort to explore the diversity of service design projects with the attendant variety in the activities of service designers, Meroni and Sangirogi (2011) analyze 17 cases of service design. They identified four main areas for design intervention—designing interactions, relations, and experiences; shaping broader systems and organizations; identifying new collaborative service models; and imagining future directions for service systems. Within each of these broad areas service designers employed a range of strategies and techniques. They borrowed "tools" from user centered and interaction design such as scenarios (Carroll, 1995; Bødker, 2000; Carroll, 2013), personas (Grudin, and Pruitt, 2002; Miaskiewicz and Kozar 2011) use cases (Morelli and Tollestrup 2009), and storytelling (Evenson, 2006), and from service marketing flow charts, blueprinting (Shostack, 1982; Bitner et al., 2008), and customer journey maps (Zomerdijk and Voss, 2010; Crosier and Handford, 2012; Følstad, et al., 2014). Depending on the design context, designers made choices about the tools and techniques most appropriate. In addition, Meroni and Sangirogi (2011) found that the starting points for the project were as diverse as the (re) design of websites, touch points, physical spaces, policies, and business models. This in turn influenced designers' relations to these "objects" of design, which varied greatly from making service concepts concrete through drawings and flowcharts to being involved in the commercialization of the service (Goldstein et al., 2002: 122).

The diverse set of activities that are bundled under the rubric of service design are too numerous for us to detail here, but nearly all involve developing visual ways of representing services to allow for the iterative refinement of service concepts and to support collaboration and communication among designers and others involved in the design process. The need for service representations is obvious, although their uses by practitioners throughout designing can be varied and frequently ambiguous.

6.3.1   REPRESENTATIONS

As we explored in Chapter 5 representation is critical in all design practices. For example, in industrial design and architecture representations, in the form of product diagrams or blueprints, are pivotal in communicating successfully with clients and product teams. For these disciplines representational skills such as drafting and drawing are necessary to good practice as representations play a key role from initial ideation and including the final drawings from which a product ultimately will be built. In these fields there is the possibility of detecting and even measuring gaps between drawings or representations and the product as produced or manufactured. In this way imagination and precision are brought together through representation. This is possible because in principle the materialization of ideas can be specified in terms the properties of the objects designed, including their locations in space and time.

Design often is described as following a process where project objectives are established first, followed by a stage of idea generation that leads to concept development, and finally concepts are fleshed out through prototypes, which may include refining concepts through feedback from users. In both concept development and prototyping designers rely on representations to explore alternatives and make refinements. These canonical steps in design also broadly describe service design, but because services are enacted and dynamically co-produced, service designers must adapt representational tools used in product design to support service design and innovation (Holmlid and Evenson, 2007).

Service designers have attempted to create representations that render abstract qualities of services more tangible, sharable, and ultimately designable. They have developed ways to represent services to help communicate intentions, enable the emergence of a shared vision for the design among key stakeholders, and assess the degree to which the service as imagined is aligned with the service as experienced. As Morelli (2002: 13) states, "The activity of design consists in the projection of a set of ideas into future configurations. Because of this, design activity heavily relies on visual representation, which is critical in communicating a project to clients, in verifying the validity of the project, and in generating a plan that can be understood and executed by other actors in the design process." However, because services are about what people do—their interactions, and the histories, skills, and other resources they bring to the service experience—it is difficult to assess the relation between abstract design representations of the service and the service as experienced or enacted. The relationship between the "critical visual representation" and an "executable plan" is neither simple nor direct, but rather, is embedded in the practices of service designers. Such representations are resources in play that can justify multiple enactments of the service and whose very ambiguity allows heterogeneous assemblages of service professionals to act together despite the lack of an *a priori* executable plan.

The difficulty in representing abstract service performances has also been noted in efforts to make services knowable and tangible to service recipients (Shostack, 1984). Designers, it is suggested, should provide tangible evidence that a service has been delivered and something of value has been produced. These tangible markers of service often are more easily represented in design specifications and may serve to stand in for the actual interactions that take place when a service is enacted. For example, noting that a toll-free number was called and answered by a service technician in a specified amount of time represents the interaction of caller and call taker, or specifying that a hotel worker greets returning guests by name denotes a design specification for hotel services. However, such representations provide only thin "data" about the complexity of the service or how participants engage with or experience the service.

Not-with-standing the challenges of representing services, two types of service representations, service blueprints and customer journey maps, have become important tools for service design. Each raises questions about the role of these artifacts in design; the ways they articulate with what people do and the material context in which they do it, including the exercise of agency and power; and finally how they are taken up and used by those who implement and enact services. Using an analogy with architecture where the architect creates the blueprint, in the realm of services, we might ask who are the structural engineers, contractors, and carpenters who bring the blueprint to life? Following Morelli (2002), who are the other actors who act upon the service blueprints and customer journey maps, and in doing so enact, adapt, and even transform the original representations?

One of the important techniques developed to help visualize services and make their descriptions more concrete is service blueprinting. The technique was introduced three decades ago by Shostack (1984) as a way to add rigor in how services were developed so that implementation problems could be identified before they occurred. The method has evolved over the years with an emphasis on the role of blueprinting in providing a customer focus to the design of services. Beyond the aim of improving service quality, blueprinting seeks to assure "a distinctive, memorable service experience" (Bitner et al., 2008: 70) by depicting customer interactions over time through different touch points.

Service blueprinting provides a methodologically structured way of presenting activities, relationships, and interdependencies through the visualization of service processes, points of customer contact, and the physical and tangible evidence associated with services from the customer's perspective. In addition, blueprints help multiple stakeholders reach consensus and manage expectations by making visible processes and activities, including the responsibilities of customers and service providers, the role of equipment and facilities, and the quality standards, expectations, and costs.

Bitner et al. (2008) define five key components of a service blueprint—customer actions; actions of front stage, customer facing employees; actions of backstage employees that are invisible to customers; support processes; and physical evidence (see Figure 6.2). The blueprint is laid out linearly and temporally from left to right starting with the first point of contact customers have with the service. At each point the actions of employees with direct contact with customers are indicated. In addition, actions that take place outside the customers' visibility, but that are necessary to deliver the service, are mapped. Finally, any physical evidence that the customer receives is depicted.

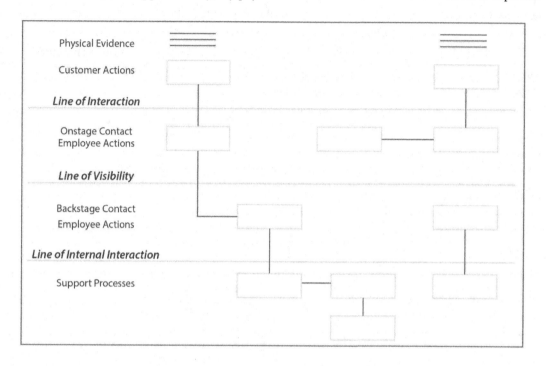

Figure 6.2: Service blueprint template. Adapted from Zeithaml et al. (2006).

Customer journey maps are similar to service blueprints as they describe the journey of service recipients as they navigate various touch points and service interfaces (Miettinen and Koivisto, 2009; Stickdorn and Schneider, 2010). The customer's interactions are described step-by-step with an emphasis on the information and the physical objects involved. The more touch points, the more complicated the map becomes. Customer journey maps, like blueprints, may be end-to-end descriptions, looking at the entire arc of a service engagement, or at other times they may focus on one aspect of the service, for example the check-in process at a hotel.

In contrast with service blueprints, customer journey maps are described as depicting "a higher level of synthesis" showing a simplified representation of the customer experience with "redundant information" and details being left out (http://www.servicedesigntools.org/tools/8). Customer journey maps typically do not include the implementation details or what an organization needs to do to implement the service. The emphasis is on the front stage customer interactions—things the customers do to engage with the service. In addition, customer journey maps are not always strictly linear as they show how customers interact with some touch points and miss others entirely or return to earlier points in the service experience. Although customer journey maps take many forms, Figure 6.3 provides an example of a customer journey map template that designers fill out to describe the experiences of customers as they engage with a service.

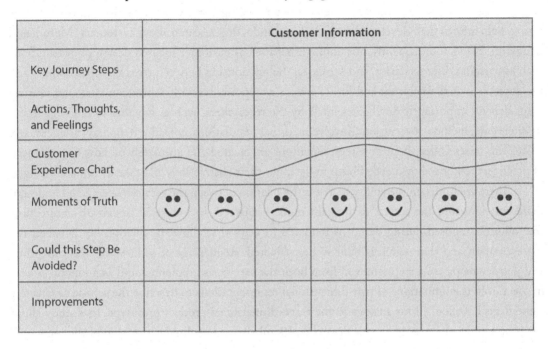

Figure 6.3: Customer journey map template. Adapted from Smart Cities—Guide to using customer journey mapping, slide 5.

One of the challenges for blueprinting and customer journey mapping is to circumscribe and precisely render the design space while at the same time not creating blinders to important design considerations—paraphrasing Bitner et al. (2008), finding a balance between closure and openness. Proponents of blueprinting caution that it is unwise to settle too quickly on a "master idea" that guides the design going forward. But as with any representation some things will be depicted in the blueprint while others will be left off the representation. Careful consideration and reflection needs to be given to what is shown in the blueprint and why, remembering that "The level of detail depicted in the blueprint is a function of the purpose for which it is being created" (Bitner et al. (2008: 73). Nonetheless, what is left out of the blueprint may be as important as what is included for differently positioned service participants.

To guide and influence the service as enacted, blueprints must ultimately be translated by those who "implement" the components of the service, including such things as the layout of the facility, the training of employees, and the tangible artifacts provided to customers such as instructions or receipts. The robustness and "completeness" of the blueprint become evident at the point of implementation when details left out of the overall blueprint may need to be added sometimes in the form of a "sub-document of the main blueprint" (Bitner et al., 2008: 71).

Service blueprinting and customer journey mapping borrow methods from interaction design to help inform their development, including conducting research about customers (Meroni and Sangiorgi, 2011). Consequently, not unlike other user or customer focused design representations such as personas, user scenarios, and use cases; the relationship between research on customers and the depictions of their current and future actions as represented in blueprints or customer journey maps depend importantly on choices made by the researchers, such as whether to rely on surveys or interviews, include observations, involve marginal populations, consider temporal variances, and so on. This raises issues about how representations are created and ultimately on how they are used in practice, the know-how needed both to decipher their abstractions and take action accordingly.

There are limits on the ability to assess the relation between the services as depicted in design representations and the service as implemented or enacted. In industrial design or architecture, the "object" proposed during design is rendered in ways that allow the relationship between the representation and that which is built to be evaluated. Renderings of services such as blueprints and journey maps are a step removed from both the service as a potential and as a kinetic system in use. Given the limitations of two-dimensional representations to describe the service as enacted, some firms have looked for analogs to the three-dimensional product prototype. In a study about the prototyping practices of service designers, Blomkvist and Holmid (2010) found the term prototyping was used rather loosely and with little consistency. At times prototyping involved using scenarios and role-playing to enact either the "whole" service or specific touch points. At other times tangible, three-dimensional elements of the service, such as facilities or service-enabling gadgets, were prototyped so users could engage with them. Designers in this study also noted the difficulty in assessing the validity of prototypes, particularly when what is being prototyped is only part of an overall service. There was no way for them to assess how those elements of the service that were not part of the prototype might ultimately interact with the the prototyped elements and effect the service experience.

Notwithstanding the difficulty of prototyping services, a few firms have started to prototype services by setting up "test" environments that provide different levels of fidelity between the experimental setting and the actual site in which the service will be delivered. For example, Bank of American turned a set of branches into "laboratories" to try out new banking services for retail banking, recognizing that "an organization's capacity to innovate relies on a process of experimentation whereby new products and services are created and existing ones improved" (Thomke, 2003: 274). If the prototyped services prove useful, they can be rolled out to other branches. Service firms such as Google, Facebook, and Yahoo regularly prototype new offerings by making service changes available to a small subset of their customer base, and depending of the results of these "experiments," the new services are offered more broadly. Prototyping these digitally delivered services are typically less costly than those that require building physical spaces and therefore can be undertaken more frequently.

Designing has always been more than creating static design representations and the relationship between these representations and the world we hope to affect through design is never simple or straightforward. We often think of design as something that occurs in a time and a place even when the temporal dimension extends over months or years and place is geographically distributed. However, because services involve performances, it is inevitable that their designing continues every time a service is enacted and a transformation occurs. The myriad ways the designed elements interact with an always dynamic and changing world cannot be predicted. This raises questions for the designer regarding the need to design for change and for the time when the designer is no longer an active participant in either enacting the service or being accountable for its outcomes (Voss et al., 2009). Because time is a key dimension in service design, approaches and skills in making temporalities enacted in projects explicit, rather than hidden are needed. Representations ultimately freeze that temporality and risk presenting the service as static and unambiguous, thereby concealing the important work that is required to realize the service as an embodied activity.

Design, like all activities, is embedded in a social milieu. The notion of a user presupposes a particular relation to that which is used just as the notion of a designer presupposes a relation to a designed entity. But we know from an extensive literature on design-in-use (Henderson and Kyng, 1991; Aanestad, 2003; Redström, 2006, 2008) that the roles of user and designer are not so easily demarcated. Problematizing the role of the designer extends the reach of design to include that which is constituted through ongoing social interactions (Clement, 1993). The conceptualization of services as co-productions and co-creations necessitates that service designers acknowledge and reflect on the limits of their role in design, including their responsibilities for service outcomes. Furthermore, the institutional and organizational positioning of the designer with respect to that which is designed defines opportunities and constraints on participation in the service and as such in its ongoing design-in-use. Akam and Prendiville (2013: 31) make a similar point when they direct us to, "re-situate services as an organic, co-created process and see co-designing as a journey and process of transformation in how we design our world, and ourselves, with others." An anthropology of services calls for an examination of the situated practices of designers and their relation to a broad range of actors who animate the service.

The sociality of services also reminds us that designers also participate in service worlds where they learn to see problems and opportunities—and construct services as their solution. They do not just discover services in the world that are then described and analyzed, much like a natural historian. Designers participate in communities of practice with their own conventions which are consequential to their ability to intervene in service worlds. Likewise, what is designed—a set of symbols, rules, specifications, models—will be enacted through similar social processes. Thus, the notion of implementing designed services is dubious, at least in a straightforward way, because our designs cannot specify all the salient adjustments and accommodations that will be made by differently positioned people as they enact and manage the service-in-use.

Recognizing that designers also participate in service worlds along with those they design with and for also has implications for how we understand the design process. Distinct starting and stopping points that often characterize the design process are typically lacking in service design. Addressing a similar issue, Ehn (2008) explores the place of participatory and meta-design in the design of *things*, conceptualized as sociomaterial arrangements. Drawing on the work of Latour (1999) and Latour and Weibel (2005), Ehn argues for understanding design as beginning before and continuing during the "design project" supported by participatory approaches. Design is also conceptualized as continuing afterwards in what Ehn (2008) refers to as meta-design, akin to design-in-use but extended to include design-for-design. Despite the ubiquitous discourse of the importance of service innovation, the various elements from which services are built have histories and as such are less *de novo* productions than modifications to on-going flows of activity. As such, the designer writ large is better understood as intervening in interactions and exchanges that are both enduring and partial.

If an anthropology of services requires that we attend to the *practices* of designers and others involved in the production of services, it also entails an obligation to examine the *positions* of designers vis-à-vis their role as designers. Practices do not arbitrarily arise as enacted, but emerge within specific sociomaterial circumstances. While we caution against proclaiming clear starting and stopping points for service design projects, we acknowledge that sales pitches, contracts, and deadlines are part of the everyday "realities" of many designers' lives. While we argue that loosely coupled ecosystems rather than precisely tooled machines provide better models for conceptualizing services, we also recognize that precise specifications of outcomes from well-bounded systems are more likely to be rewarded in many situations, even when everyone involved accepts that the promise of control is illusory. We do not suggest that these conditions in which designers operate are always dysfunctional or that it can be entirely supplanted with a practice approach. An anthropology of services built on attention to practices is offered as a necessary corrective to design conventions and expectations that divert attention from the very real conditions within which the transformations offered by service designers are developed, maintained, and modified. An anthropology of services is not simply an approach to design that fits into extant ways of doing business. It has implications for the position of designers and the allocation of skills and power within design projects.

6.4   FROM DESIGN TO ASSEMBLAGE

Given the broad range of concerns that potentially are implicated in realizing service outcomes, it is perhaps more fruitful to think of services as less designed than assembled from the sociomaterial arrangements available and those yet to be fashioned. Service designers then might be advised to locate themselves in relation to these entities and work out in what ways they are accountable to the people and organizations who are involved in facilitating desired service outcomes. And this highlights the fact that—perhaps more explicitly than in other design fields—service design is both ethical and political. As such, service designers cannot ignore that design choices have consequences for who is included in defining outcomes and the ways to achieve them, and who benefits if or when the outcomes are achieved. A key challenge for designers is to develop an orientation to the work they do and the choices embedded in their tools and methods that recognizes that service outcomes necessarily endorse and validate some interests and people over others.

Our discussion of service design is not conducted as critique, but as a way to explore opportunities to further develop the field. For example, there is a need for ways to describe the worlds into which services are integrated, as well as strategies for conceptualizing the inherent indeterminacy of services in ways that can support considered action. New ways of conceptualizing and representing services are needed to better determine what elements of design are relevant where and why, and with what implications for the skills and knowledge of all the actors involved in enacting the service. Finally, we suggest that the field needs a connoisseurship of services so that their producers and consumers appreciate the value of partial, selective interventions into service worlds instead of fixating on illusory whole service systems.

CHAPTER 7

An Anthropology of Services

7.1 JOURNEY'S END

As our journey is at its end, we may now fairly ask where have we arrived and how did we get here. Regarding the latter, our approach has been anthropological both in order to situate services and design in society and to participate in service design. Ever the anthropologists, we not only explore a phenomenon of interest, but simultaneously problematize or question the very concepts used to understand it. Indeed, we never take for granted that the phenomena we study exist in pristine form independent of our attempts to conceptualize and understand them. Our approach has accordingly been to treat the concepts of services and service design as constructs that have meaning within particular social milieus while simultaneously situating them in the human condition. Understanding services, their variety, and their origins obliges the lengthy time horizons and cultural comparisons taken for granted by anthropologists.

Our destination is defined by a core concept in anthropology and other social sciences, namely that of practices. By adopting a practice approach we explicitly shift from propositional knowledge to the know-how embodied in actions, including those of creating services. We claim that this shift helps us distinguish between the confident and definitive language of service science and design and the ambiguity and conceptual untidiness of bringing about services. Our intention has been to clarify and develop concepts that respect designing in services as being about a know-how that draws together basic themes of social analysis and linking them to human betterment, as difficult as the latter is to define.

7.2 PACKING THE RUCKSACK

So our journey is less at an end than at a pause as we consider what to pack in our rucksacks for what lies ahead. The equipment we take guarantees neither an uneventful trip nor automatic success. In fact, a basic lesson is that it is risky to reduce service designing to technique, as reassuring as mastery of clear and explicit steps can be. Instead, a practice approach requires a questioning frame of mind and willingness to explore and challenge assumptions. We suggest that such an approach is necessary anytime we wish to design services with the goal of human betterment and that taking short cuts on the way can inadvertently lengthen the trip or alter where we find ourselves at its end.

7.2.1   HUMAN CONDITION

Services are part of being human and always have been. Services are erected atop our common humanity and explicit design is but one influence in how services come about. Although the sociotechnical conditions in which services are enacted are varied and have changed overtime, the capacity to transform the world of people, artifacts, spaces, and information through human action and interaction is at the core of how we as a species have always gotten on. So we speak of services as part of the human condition.

The diversity of the human experience reminds us that our lives always could be lived in ways other than they are; there are many ways to be human. The plasticity in the ways humans have adapted derives from our capacity to conceptualize the world and act intentionally in it, instead of just behaving. However, the costs and benefits of how we adapt are not uniform and may play out unequally. This reminds us that service concepts are constructs of particular times and places that both reflect what we think is important and shape how we look at the world and identify what is interesting. The concepts we impose on the world are necessary for us to see and understand services, but they also shape our ideas about what is important and blind us to other ways of looking. This means that services and their design can always be conceptualized and undertaken in different ways.

7.2.2   A PRACTICE LENS

The human condition requires concepts that capture its distinctive character, especially the agency with which we engage the world. This means focusing on how people, including designers, *act* in the world. Such an approach locates sociality in practices or "materially mediated arrays of human activity centrally organized around shared practical understanding" (Schatzki, 2001: 2). Practices contribute to order in the absence of rational decision making and they provide analytic flexibility to examine phenomena as diverse as communities, societies, governments, corporations, and families. A practice approach emphasizes practical understanding where shared and diverse skills and explicit propositions work jointly, and it allows non-human "agents" such as technological devices to be treated as legitimate participants in human action.

A practice lens provides a way to look at what people do in the world and at the order it expresses and enacts. It situates what people do in networks of significance rather than in discretely bounded systems. People are not viewed as merely following scripts, but are activity engaged in enacting the world they inhabit through their practices. A practice approach disentangles activity from accounts and explanations of it. But it also situates service designing as just another field of practices and in doing so it embeds designing in the social world. It points to the gap between services as they are described and represented and as they are animated through practices. Services as fundamentally abstract propositions or transformations are replaced with sociomaterial configurations of people and their know-how, artifacts, and spaces. In this way services are embedded within practices and are animated through practices.

7.2.3   RESEARCH

Viewing services as embedded in the human condition demands humility and tolerance of ambiguity; the human condition does not reveal itself in tidy categories. We must look beyond what we think we already know to be salient and challenge our assumptions about what is relevant. The complex milieus into which designers expect to place their designs means finding and following unexpected leads without knowing what counts or necessarily how to count it. Additionally, knowing the limits of research is important since ultimately designing services is about going beyond the present and attempting to create something that does not currently exist—a transformation and the conditions that make it happen.

Consequently, the "purposes" for research vary and they are not simply about discovery of a "need" for new services, but also about enabling imagination and creativity. In this way, we can be taken far from what would seem to be the immediate design challenge. For example, Ljungblad and Holmquist (2007) conducted research into the practices of owners of pets who respond minimally to their human owners (e.g. reptiles and insects) to inform the design of robots. The logic of transfer scenarios grounds design in practices that are seemingly marginal to immediate design goals, but which can nudge thinking into new directions.

An approach that is broadly ethnographic where the researchers position themselves more as learners than experts is well suited to explore the sociotechnical locales and situations where services are enacted and evolve. Ethnography can be visualized as a funneling process in which fieldworkers start with open-ended observations and conversations that shift through a learning process to more structured research strategies and techniques. Ethnography is sufficiently flexible to allow fieldworkers to address questions that are relevant to them and the people they are studying. This flexibility facilitates moving from fine-grained analyses of people's day-to-day activities to broader societal conditions and trends.

Ethnographic studies involve fieldwork in "real-world" settings. These designated "field sites," be they actual physical spaces or conceptual are an obvious and essential component of all ethnographic research Recently, the notion of field site has been extended to include so-called "multi-sited" studies where the conventional view of "locality" as spatially and temporally bounded is replaced with a view of the field site as constituted by mobility, intersection, and flow; with a focus on connections, associations, and relationships across space and time. In this sense, "the field site is ... reflexively constructed by every choice the ethnographer makes in selecting, connecting, and bounding the site and via the interactions through which s/he engages with the material artifacts and the people who define the field" (Blomberg and Karasti, 2013: 389).

Ethnography allows us to describe in detail the material configurations in which people act, and in which services are enacted. Attention is directed toward the perspectives of different participants in order to reflect insider perspectives and their relation to the categories of outside communities of scholars, such as ethnographers. While there are many well-established ethnographic research techniques and strategies, ethnography is more than a collection of techniques or a methodology (Blomberg and Burrell, 2012). It is about creating a narrative, a story that is sensible and, for our practice approach, ultimately *useful* for designing. This means it is also important that the interests and abilities of those with whom ethnographers collaborate in designing be taken into consideration.

Finally, the relational quality and holistic focus in anthropology directs ethnographers to the larger societal implications of people's practices. As such research about something as seemingly mundane as green beans might lead to understanding trends in nutrition and health care, but also in spirituality and climate change. Insights from ethnographic studies do not map directly onto design specifications or straightforwardly generate design requirements. They must be connected and integrated with design agendas and practices, recognizing "the importance of creating the conditions in which design can draw on insights" from research on people's practices (Blomberg and Burrell, 2012: 1044).

7.2.4   DISCOURSE OF SERVICES

It is difficult to point to services like we can objects. Architect Frank Lloyd Wright could point to Fallingwater and pronounce "house" or industrial designer Philippe Stark could lift a spider-like sculpture and proclaim "juicer," and importantly others could respectfully disagree. Services cannot be pointed to in the same way and so they are constructed through discourse that links interactions and performances to something identified as a service. Service discourse is not only *about* the service, but it looms large in the constitution of it. How we talk about services is prominent in the practices of making a service real and identifiable.

Through discourse services are constructed as bounded, distinct systems with encounters that distinguish them from the rest of the world. Consensus about a service is not guaranteed, but it is through discourse that different points of view are expressed and negotiated. Through influence and control of the discourse "official" definitions of the service are promulgated and some characteristics of the service and how it came to be are privileged, while others remain unarticulated and thus invisible to many. Arguments constructed through discourse define appropriate users of the service and the minimal personal skills and attitudes necessary for proper usage, thereby screening out some potential users. Definitions of human betterment that underlie designing are invariably built through discourse, including dialogue and debate, as are metrics by which a service is designated as efficient and effective. Even the transformations facilitated by the service are negotiated through words in order to be recognized as something other than ineluctable personal experience.

Just as discourse "reveals" services, it also can direct attention away from what else is happening, leaving some people and activities in the shadows. By attending to the discourse of services we are reminded of the limitation of discourse to create or enact the service as defined. The service and how we know it are never final and complete. There is always much that is not denoted in words and nods of mutual agreement. Even as people enact services through practices, with all the commonality implied, in the end the "service" must be experienced. As such we are mindful that while the discourse of service may seemingly provide a kind of closure and agreement, ambiguity and openness to redefinition loom in the background.

7.2.5   INTERVENING AND ASSEMBLING

A practice approach assumes that activity is always ongoing and open to intervention and change, where artifacts are introduced, activities are shifted to new sites, the sequence or duration of activities change, and different people become involved. By focusing on designing as intervention instead of as *de novo* creation we are reminded that acts of design are ubiquitous accompaniments to social life and the latter carries enormous momentum. From the point of view of those just getting on with their lives, explicit acts of design may be unnoticed or without significant consequence.

Designing as intervening is less about the brilliant designer/creator than it is about people who are knowledgeable about practices and the histories they build upon, and who draw upon that knowledge to leverage existing practices for new possibilities. Intervening implies continuity and adjustment, with an emphasis on helping people "get on" with everyday life instead of as innovation that brings about radical breaks with the past. Accordingly, interventions necessarily involve assembling existing elements in new ways and with new components to bring about change.

The emphasis on intervening and assembling points to the importance of time in designing, both its duration and how it becomes divided into categories often depicted as steps. A practice approach asks us to reconsider how service design is typically presented as a project with clear starting and stopping points and a time-based division of labor where designing and prototyping are temporally organized into stages that imply expertise and distinct roles. A practice approach recognizes that service designing is best thought of not as a clearly bounded activity, separable from the rest of life with only a few adjustments occurring to the service as designed. The "designers" in all their forms will be there long after the explicit design project has ended. By emphasizing intervention and assembly, the practice lens extends the duration of design and makes engaging with and reworking the "new" service an ordinary aspect of designing and not a sign of poor or incomplete design. The appropriate analogy for service design may be of shiatsu with its repeated application of pressure to key points on the body rather than the sudden and jarring adjustments of a chiropractor.

Looking at designing as intervention and assembly exposes the service designer to new relationships where they encounter potentially unfamiliar practices that involve the designer in animating elements of the service. The assumption of *de novo* creation rests on the myth that elements of the service can be designed and configured without attention to history. A practice approach connects the designer to a panoply of practices that are themselves situated in time. In this way service designing is best understood as an open process with no necessary beginnings or endings or fixed hand-offs between stages.

7.2.6   POLITICS OF DESIGN

Services are often described as co-produced and it is a short and risky step to interpret this as a kind of harmonious endeavor in which everyone knows and accepts their roles and pulls together to produce the service with value emanating to all. But services are structured in ways where those involved in enacting the service are differently and sometimes only loosely tethered to the "owners" of the service. Efforts to make those who deliver services, for example wait-staff, janitors, or nurses, perform in ways deemed necessary or efficient by the service firms for whom they work are ubiquitous. While there may be a kind of optimism in co-production discourse as it implies working together, the very openness in what co-production can imply warrants careful scrutiny. Services can be viewed as sites for contestations where freedom or autonomy play out in relation to predictability and control. The contests vary with the service, as do the interests, influence, and authority being exercised. Cleavages can exist between consumers, service employees, and providers, and also between people and machines that define and limit the service. Co-production does not guarantee that the services we design and enact will not result in dystopian futures.

There are politics in services and their design, as assumptions about who is entitled to what are exercised and where the "scripts" for co-production are written and revised. Human betterment—what it is and how it is achieved—is always based on some, but not all, voices being heard. Because the services we design and enable are world making, we cannot dodge the issue of service politics. Accordingly, we must ask what interests are at play, why are they at play, who is heard (and not), and above all, who will reap the benefits and bear any costs, intended or not.

7.2.7   VALUE

Just as co-production has its politics, so does co-creation have its values. Service designers emphasize that the value of a service is co-created jointly in interactions between service providers and recipients. The quest for the right value proposition is commonplace in the service literature with the assumption that value results from a mutually beneficial relationship. If the correct value proposition can be found service providers can move potential recipients into becoming actual value co-creators. However, the qualities that are valued in use have different meanings to those involved in enacting the service. While for services to be sustained they must be valued, there is much more to valuing than can be summed up in cost-benefit analysis or win-win propositions.

If service is essentially about mobilizing resources to enable some, but not all, transformations to occur, then service is fundamentally about exercising values. Services make sense within specific social and cultural contexts, and participation in a service may align with the values of some, while possibly simultaneously infringing on the values of others. It is a mistake to conclude that everyone agrees on the "co-created" value of a service. Agreeing on what is valuable about a service encounter is not a prerequisite to action. But services can be reminders of whose values count and in what ways under different conditions. A practice approach provides conceptual tools for tackling these broader questions of how value is established.

7.2.8   OUTCOMES

A practice approach to service designing favors humility and modesty in considering the designer's capacity to deliver a service system or component of it that can be "started up" to produce its intended effects. The question of whether the service system "works" is overly simplistic, assuming that there is a way to arrive at an agreed upon definition of what it means to "work" apart from consideration of the potentially diverse perspectives of service participants, not to mention those who are affected without being directly involved or explicitly aware of the service. A service may work in the narrow sense of producing its intended transformation, but in doing so it may affect the lives of a great many people who are oblivious to their connection to service outcomes.

Services such as child care, elder care, or recreation can be commodified and thereby disrupt traditional roles within families and communities. They can also transfer skill from the consumer to the producer and vise versa. For example, interior design services can result in both more elegant and functional dwellings, and occupants who are less confident in their own taste. Conversely, interior design technologies and online services can make homeowners into interior designers with a pallet of possible design options to mix and match. The point is not that this is harmful or good or bad, but it is a very real consequence of services. It is all too easy to dismiss these effects as "unintended consequences" as if the absence of intent explains them or makes them tolerable. A practice approach is concerned with outcomes, which themselves are always evolving, and how they reverberate in the world. Those involved in designing services cannot dismiss inadvertent outcomes as collateral damage or manna from heaven, but rather view them as the result of our intervening in the world by reassembling what we find there. The point is significant for by blurring the line between what is intended or not we can look directly at the results of our intervening. And while we may not be able to realize our intentions through service design, we can strive to make some outcomes more or less likely. What this form of service designing lacks in glamor is more than made up for through the marginal changes that incrementally hold the promise of making things better over time.

7.3   ONWARD

Service worlds and service design can benefit from a practice approach to designing services, one that is broadly anthropological. While much work remains, the steps ahead are guided by the view that the anthropological record of documenting diverse ways of life can contribute to how we conceptualize and engage with services. By assuming that services past and present are embedded in a social context, we can simultaneously identify resources that the designer of services can draw upon while better recognizing the limits or constraints on any effort to design services. In addition, anthropological perspectives on services push us to consider our own practices as members of communities of practice working within specific organizations and communities. This focus on designing services is fundamentally about designers' relationships to other people, both real and imagined, past and present. The emphasis is on what sorts of institutions are implied by conceptualizing service design in particular ways and how and in what ways those institutions include anthropologists.

Furthermore, a practice approach to designing services argues that people, including designers, populate a world that has been largely designed and built by others and as such the scope for design is both ubiquitous and restricted. Accordingly, service designers must take into consideration that the people they are designing for are already tinkering with their own lives and are always participants in the work of design. Designing then is achieved in fragments and involves managing unintended consequences at the limits of efficacy and power. Finally, the question of values in designing is far more complex than that of finding a good value proposition in the business sense. While services are frequently conceptualized from the perspectives of business and information technology professionals, this delimits the focus of design, presupposes the skills and knowledge deemed relevant to designing services, and can lead to ignoring how the costs and benefits of adopting new services are borne by different members of society writ large.

The call then is to portray everyday life and how it might be different than it is, how ordinary people design in ways that may be ubiquitous and yet unrecognized, and how designers enact the activities they believe constitute design. The challenge for a practice approach to designing services is to explicate the assumptions, concepts, values, and methods that today seem commonplace and to contribute a discourse that does not assume or naturalize a particular approach to what it means to design services. The result will situate services fully as part of the human condition and as a proper topic for the anthropological gaze.

Bibliography

Aanestad, M. (2003). The camera as an actor: Design-in-use of telemedicine infrastructure in surgery. *Computer-Supported Cooperative Work* (CSCW), 12: 1–20. DOI: 10.1023/A:1022492210898. 69

Akam, Y. and Prendville, A. (2013). Embodying, enacting and entangling design: A phenomenological view to co-designing services. *Swedish Design Research Journal*, 1 (13): 29–40. DOI: 10.3384/svid.2000-964X.13129#sthash.xOvlqzek.dpuf. 69

Åkesson, M., Skålén, P., and Edvardsson, B. (2008). E-government and service orientation: gaps between theory and practice. *International Journal of Public Sector Management*, 21(1): 74–92. DOI: 10.1108/09513550810846122. 12

Alexander, C. (1964). *Notes on the Synthesis of Form.* Cambridge, MA: Harvard University Press. 49

Alter, S. (2008). Service system fundamentals: Work system, value chain, and life cycle. *IBM Systems Journal*, 47(1): 71–85. DOI: 10.1147/sj.471.0071. 42

Arthur, W. B. (2011). The second economy. *McKinsey Quarterly*, 4: 90–99. 19

Basole, R. C. and Rouse, W. B. (2008). Complexity of service value networks: Conceptualization and empirical investigation. *IBM Systems Journal*, 47(1): 53–70. DOI: 10.1147/sj.471.0053. 42

Belk, R. (2013). You are what you can access: Sharing and collaborative consumption online. *Journal of Business Research.* Available online. DOI: 10.1016/j.jbusres.2013.10.001.

Berlingieri, G. (2013). Outsourcing and the rise in services. CEP Discussion Paper No 1199, April 2013. 13

Berry, L. L. (1995). Relationship marketing of services—growing interest, emerging perspectives. *Journal of the Academy of Marketing Science*, 23(4): 236–245. DOI: 10.1177/009207039502300402. 35

Bijker, W. E., Hughes, T. P., and Pinch, T., J. (Eds.) (1987). *The Social Construction of Technological Systems: New Directions in the Sociology and History of Technology.* Cambridge, MA: MIT press. 30

Bijker, W. E. and Law, J. (1992). *Shaping Technology/Building Society: Studies in Sociotechnical Change.* Cambridge, MA: MIT press. 30

Bitner, M. J., Ostrom, A. L., and Morgan, F. N. (2008). Service blueprinting: a practical technique for service innovation. *California Management Review*, 50(3): 66–94. DOI: 10.2307/41166446. 57, 63, 65, 67, 68

Bitner, M. J., Faranda, W. T., Hubbert, A. R. and Zeithaml, V. A. (1997). Customer contributions and roles in service delivery. *International Journal of Service Industry Management*, 8 (3): 193–205. DOI: 10.1108/09564239710185398. 37

Blomberg, J. (1988). The variable impact of computer technologies on the organization of work activities. In *Computer-Supported Cooperative Work*: *A Book of Readings*, I. Greif, Ed. San Mateo, CA: Morgan Kaufman Publisher: 771–782. 30

Blomberg, J. (2008). Negotiating meaning of shared information in service system encounters. *European Management Journal*, 26(4): 213–222. DOI: 10.1016/j.emj.2008.05.004. xiii, 4

Blomberg, J. (2009). On participation and service innovation, In *(Re-) searching a Digital Bauhaus*, Binder, T., Löwgren, J. and Malmborg, L., Eds., Springer: 121–144. 59

Blomberg, J. (2010). Work in the service economy. In *Introduction to service engineering* Karwowski, W. and Salvendy, G., Eds. Hoboken, NJ: Wiley and Sons, Inc.: 48–70. 20

Blomberg, J. (2011). Trajectories of Change in Global Enterprise Transformation. In *Ethnographic Praxis in Industry Conference Proceedings*: 134–151. xiii. 4

Blomberg, J. and Burrell M. (2012). An ethnographic approach to design. In *Human–Computer Interaction Handbook: Fundamentals, Evolving Technologies, and Emerging Applications*, Jacko, J. A., Ed. Boca Raton, FL: CRC Press: 1025–1052. DOI: 10.1201/b11963-52. 76

Blomberg, J. and Downs, C. (2014). Service Design and the Emergence of a Second Economy. In *Mapping and developing Service Design Research in the UK*, Sangiorgi, D., Prendiville, A., and Rickettes, A. Eds. SDR: Service Design Research Network. (available at www.servicedesignresearch.com/uk/): 50–51. 16

Blomberg, J. and Evenson, S. (2006). Service innovation and design. In *CHI'06 Extended Abstracts on Human Factors in Computing Systems*. ACM: 28–31. DOI: 10.1145/1125451.1125460. 59

Blomberg, J., Suchman, L., and Trigg, R. H. (1996). Reflections on a work-oriented design project. *Human-Computer Interaction*, 11(3): 237–265. DOI: 10.1207/s15327051hci1103_3. xiii, 4

Blomberg, J., Suchman, L., and Trigg, R. (1997). Back to work: Renewing old agendas for cooperative design. In *Computers and Design in Context*, Mathiassen, L., Ed. Cambridge: MIT press: 268–287. xiii, 4

Blomberg, J. and Karasti, H. (2012). Positioning ethnography within participatory design. In *Routledge International Handbook of Participatory Design*, Simonsen, J. and Robertson, T., Eds. Routledge: London: 86–116.

Blomberg, J. and Karasti, H. (2013). Reflections on 25 years of ethnography in CSCW. *Computer Supported Cooperative Work* (CSCW), 22(4-6): 373–423. DOI: 10.1007/s10606-012-9183-1. 75

Blomberg, J. and Kimbell, L. (2014). The Object of Service Design. In *Mapping and developing Service Design Research in the UK*, Sangiorgi, D., Prendiville, A., and Rickettes, A. Eds. SDR: Service Design Research Network. (available at www.servicedesignresearch.com/uk/): 30–31. 61

Blomberg, J., Cefkin, M., and Rankin, Y. (2010). Mapping and visualizing service provider and client interactions: the case for participation. In *Proceedings of the 11th Biennial Participatory Design Conference*. ACM: 294–296. DOI: 10.1145/1900441.1900515.

Blomberg, J., and Darrah, C. (2015). Toward an anthropology of services. *The Design Journal*, 18(2): 171–192. xiii

Blomkvist, J. and Holmlid, S. (2010). Service prototyping according to service design practitioners. In *Proceeding of ServDes 2010*, Holmlid, S., Nisula, J-V., and Clatworthy, S., Eds. Linköping; Sweden; December 1-3, 2010. 68

Bødker, S. (2000). Scenarios in user-centred design—setting the stage for reflection and action. *Interacting with Computers*, 13(1): 61–75. DOI: 10.1016/S0953-5438(00)00024-2. 63

Bourdieu, P. (1977). *Outline of a Theory of Practice*. Cambridge: Cambridge University Press. DOI: 10.1017/CBO9780511812507. 2

Bryson, J. R., Daniels, P. W., and Warf, B. (2004). *Service Worlds: People, Organizations, Technologies*. London, UK: Routledge. 13, 20

Bubandt, N. and Otto, T. (2010). Anthropology and the Predicaments of Holism. In *Experiments in Holism: Theory and Practice in Contemporary Anthropology*, Otto, T. and Bubandt N., Eds. West Sussex, UK: Wiley-Blackwell. DOI: 10.1002/9781444324426.ch1. 43

Buchanan, R. (2001). Design research and the new learning. *Design Issues*, 17(4), 3–23. DOI: 10.1162/07479360152681056. 46

Buxton, B. (2007). *Sketching User Experiences: Getting the Design Right and the Right Design*. Morgan Kaufmann. 45

Campbell, N., O'Driscoll, A. and Saren, M. (2012). Reconceptualizing resources: A critique of service-dominate logic. *37th Annual Macromarketing Conference*, Berlin. DOI: 10.1177/0276146713497755. 37

Carroll, J. M. (1995). *Scenario-based design: envisioning work and technology in system development.* 63

Carroll, J. M. (2013). Co-production scenarios for mobile time banking. In *End-User Development.* Berlin Heidelberg: Springer: 137–152. DOI: 10.1007/978-3-642-38706-7_11. 17, 63

CBS Radio Inc. (2013). Silicon Valley's Homeless Turning To Public Transit For Shelter. Accessed at: http://sanfrancisco.cbslocal.com/2013/12/03/silicon-valleys-homeless-turning-to-public-transit-for-shelter/ (accessed 7 January 2015). 31

Cefkin, M., Thomas, J. O., and Blomberg, J. (2007). The implications of enterprise-wide pipeline management tools for organizational relations and exchanges. In *Proceedings of the 2007 International ACM Conference on Supporting Group Work.* ACM: 61–68. DOI: 10.1145/1316624.1316634. 4

Clatworthy, S. (2011). Service innovation through touch-points: Development of an innovation toolkit for the first stages of new service development. *International Journal of Design,* 5(2): 15–28. 39, 60

Clement, A. (1993). Looking for the designers: Transforming the 'invisible' infrastructure of computerized office work. *AI and Society, Special Issue on Gender, Culture and Technology,* 7: 323–344. DOI: 10.1007/BF01891415. 69

Clement, A. and Van den Besselaar, P. (1993). A retrospective look at PD projects. *Communications of the ACM,* 36(6), 29–37. DOI: 10.1145/153571.163264. 58

Clifford J. and Marcus, G. E. (1986). *Writing Culture: The Poetics and Politics of Ethnography.* Berkeley, CA: University of California Press. 43

Crosier, A. and Handford, A. (2012). Customer journey mapping as an advocacy tool for disabled people: a case study. *Social Marketing Quarterly,* 18(1): 67–76. DOI: 10.1177/1524500411435483. 63

Cross, N. (2007). *Designerly Ways of Knowing.* Basel: Birkhauser. 48

Darrah, C. N. (1992). Workplace skills in context. *Human Organization,* 51(3): 264–273. 4

Darrah, C. (1997). Complicating the concept of skill requirements: Scenes from a workplace. *Changing work, changing workers: Critical perspectives on language, literacy and skills:* 249–272. xiii, 4

Darrah, C. N. (2006). Ethnography and working families. *The work and family handbook: multi-disciplinary perspectives and approaches:* 367–385. 4

Darrah, C. N., Freeman, J. M., and English-Lueck, J. A. (2007). *Busier than Ever!: Why American Families Can't Slow Down.* Stanford, CA: Stanford University Press. 4, 5

Darrah, C. N. (2007). The anthropology of busyness. *Human Organization*, 66(3), 261–269. xiii

Darrah, C. N., English-Lueck, J. A., and Saveri, A. (1997). The infomated households project. *Practicing Anthropology*, 19(4): 18–22. 4

Davis. H. (1999). *The Culture of Building.* New York: Oxford University Press. 51

Dervojeda, K., Verzijl, D., Nagtegaal, F., Lengton, M., and Rouwmaat, E. (2014). Design for Innovation: Service design as a means to advance business models. *Business Innovation Observatory*, European Union, February. 57

Dubberly, H. and Evenson, S. (2010). Designing for service: Creating an experience advantage. In *Introduction to Service Engineerin,g* Karwowski, W. and Salvendy, G., Eds. Hoboken, NJ: Wiley and Sons: 403–413. 55, 62

Edgett, S. and Parkinson, S. (1993). Marketing for service industries-A review. *Service Industries Journal*, 13(3): 19–39. DOI: 10.1080/02642069300000048. 35

Edvardsson, B., Gustafsson, A., and Roos, I. (2005). Service portraits in service research: a critical review. *International Journal of Service Industry Management*, 16(1): 107–121. DOI: 10.1108/09564230510587177.

Edvardsson, B., Tronvoll, B., and Gruber, T. (2011). Expanding understanding of service exchange and value co-creation: a social construction approach. *Journal of the Academic Marketing Society*, 39: 327–339. DOI: 10.1007/s11747-010-0200-y.

Ehn, P. (2008). Participation in design things. *Proceedings of Participatory Design Conference.* Bloomington, In: ACM: 92–101. 70

Emergence Conference (2006). Carnegie Mellon School of Design, Sept. 8-10. http://www.cmu.edu/PR/releases06/060808_conference.html (accessed January 25, 2015). 59

Evenson, S. (2006). Directed storytelling: Interpreting experience for design. In *Design Studies: Theory and Research in Graphic Design* Bennett, A., Ed. Princeton Architectural Press: 231–240. 63

Følstad, A., Kvale, K., and Halvorsrud, R. (2014). Customer journeys: Involving customers and internal resources in the design and management of services. In *Proceeding of Fourth Service Design and Innovation Conference.* 63

Frenkel, S., Korczynski, M., Shire, K. A., and Tam, M. (1999). *On the Front Line: Organization of Work in the Information Economy.* Cornell: Cornell University Press. 19

Gadrey, J. and Gallouj, F. (Eds.). (2002). *Productivity, Innovation and Knowledge in Services: New Economic and Socio-Economic Approaches.* Edward Elgar Publishing. DOI: 10.4337/9781781950203. 57

Garfinkel, H. (1967). *Studies in Ethnomethodology,* Englewood Cliffs, NJ: Prentice Hall. 3

George, W. R. and Berry, L. L. (1981). Guidelines for the advertising of services. *Business Horizons,* 24 (July–August): 52–56. DOI: 10.1016/0007-6813(81)90056-2. 11

Giddens, A. (1979). *Central Problems in Social Theory: Action, Structure and Contradiction in Social Analysis.* Berkeley: University of California Press. 2

Global Employment Trends (2014). *Risk of a Jobless Recovery?* International labor Office. Geneva: ILO. 13

Glusko, R. J. (2010). Seven contexts for service design. In *Handbook of Service Science,* Paul P. Maglio, Cheryl A. Kieliszewski, and James C. Spohrer, Eds. New York: Springer Verlag: 219–250. 40

Goldstein, S. M., Johnston, R., Duffy, J., and Rao, J. (2002). The service concept: the missing link in service design research?. *Journal of Operations Management,* 20(2): 121–134. DOI: 10.1016/S0272-6963(01)00090-0. 57, 63

Greenbaum and M. Kyng (Eds.) (1991). *Design at Work: Cooperative Design of Computer Systems,* Hillsdale, NJ: Lawrence Erlbaum Associates. 59

Grönroos, C. (1984). A service quality model and its marketing implications. *European Journal of Marketing,* 18(4): 36–44. DOI: 10.1108/EUM0000000004784. 33

Grönroos, C. (2006). Adopting a service logic for marketing. *Marketing Theory,* 6(3): 317–333. DOI: 10.1177/1470593106066794. 38

Grönroos, C. (2011). A service perspective on business relationships: The value creation, interaction and marketing interface. *Industrial Marketing Management,* 40(3): 240–247. DOI: 10.1016/j.indmarman.2010.06.036. 36, 37, 38

Grönroos, C. and Ojasalo, K. (2004). Service productivity: towards a conceptualization of the transformation of inputs into economic results in services. *Journal of Business Research,* 57(4): 414–423. DOI: 10.1016/S0148-2963(02)00275-8. 57

Grudin, J. and Pruitt, J. (2002). Personas, participatory design and product development: An infrastructure for engagement. In *Proceeding of Participatory Design Conference*: 144–152. 63

Gummesson, E. (1987). The new marketing—developing long-term interactive relationships. *Long Range Planning,* 20(4): 10–20. DOI: 10.1016/0024-6301(87)90151-8. 33

Gummesson, E. (2008). Extending the service-dominant logic: from customer centricity to balanced centricity. *Journal of the Academy of Marketing Science*, 36(1), 15–17. DOI: 10.1007/s11747-007-0065-x. 38

Gunn, W. and Donovan, J. (Eds.) (2012a). *Design and Anthropology*. Burlington: Ashgate.

Gunn, W. and Donovan. J. (2012b). "Design Anthropology: An Introduction." Pp 1-16. In Wendy Gunn and Jared Donovan, eds. (2012). *Design and Anthropology*. Burlington VT: Ashgate.

Gustafsson, A. and Johnson, M. D. (2003). *Competing in a Service Economy: How to Create a Competitive Advantage Through Service Development and Innovation*. San Francisco, CA: Jossey-Bass. 43

Hall, C. M. and Tucker, H. (Eds.) (2004). *Tourism and Postcolonialism: Contested Discourses, Identities and Representations*. Abingdon: Routledge. 37

Hanser, A. (2008). *Service Encounters: Class, Gender, and the Market for Social Distinction in Urban China*. Stanford, CA: Stanford University Press. 41

Harrell, S. (1997). *Human Families*. Boulder, CO: Westview. 28, 29

Hassenzahl, M. (2010). *Experience Design: Technology for All the Right Reasons*. Synthesis Lectures on Human-Centered Informatics, Morgan and Claypool Publishers, 3(1): 1–95. DOI: 10.2200/S00261ED1V01Y201003HCI008. 45

Henderson, A. and Kyng, M. (1991). There's no place like home: continuing design in use. In *Design at Work: Cooperative Design of Computer Systems*, Greenbaum, J. and Kyng, M., Eds. Hilldale, NJ: Lawrence Erlbaum Associated: 219–240. 69

Heritage, J. (1984). *Garfinkel and Ethnomethodology*, Cambridge: Polity Press. 3

Herzenberg, S.A., Alic, J.A., and Wial, H. (1998). *New Rules for a New Economy: Employment and Opportunity in a Postindustrial America*. Century Foundation. Ithaca, NY: Cornell University Press. 19

Hirose, A. and Kei-Ho Pih, K. (2011). 'No Asians working here': racialized otherness and authenticity in gastronomical Orientalism. *Ethnic and Racial Studies*, (34)9: 1482–1501. DOI: 10.1080/01419870.2010.550929. 37

Hochschild, A. (1983). *The Managed Heart. Commercialization of Human Feeling*. Berkeley, CA: University of California Press. 41

Holmlid, S. (2007). Interaction design and service design: Expanding a comparison of design disciplines. *Design Inquiries*. Stockholm: www.nordes.org. 60, 64

Holmlid, S. and Evenson, S. (2007). Prototyping and enacting services: Lessons learned from human-centered methods. *Proceedings from the 10th Quality in Services Conference*, QUIS 10. Orlando, Florida, June 14–17.

Johnson, A. W. and Earle, T. (1987). *The Evolution of Human Societies: From Foraging Group to Agrarian State*. Stanford, CA: Stanford University Press. 11, 26, 29

Karwowski, W. and Salvendy, G. (2010). *Introduction to Service Engineering*. Hoboken, NJ: Wiley and Sons, Inc. 12

Kensing, F. and Blomberg, J. (1998). Participatory design: Issues and concerns. *Computer Supported Cooperative Work* (CSCW), 7(3–4): 167–185. DOI: 10.1023/A:1008689307411. 58, 59

Kimbell, L. (2009). Insights from service design practice. *Proceedings of 8th European Academy of Design Conference*, Aberdeen, UK, April 1–3: 249–253. Available at http://ead09.rgu. ac.uk/papers.html. 55

Kimbell, L. (2011). Designing for service as one way of designing services. *International Journal of Design*, 5(2): 41–52. 55, 60

King, K. M., Sanguins, J., McGregor, L., and LeBlanc, P. (2007). First Nations People's challenge in managing coronary artery disease risk. *Qualitative Health Research*, 17(8): 1074–1087. DOI: 10.1177/1049732307307918. 40

Kingery, W. D. (2001). The design process as a critical component of the anthropology of technology. In Schiffer, M. B. (Ed.) *Anthropological Perspectives on Technology*, UNM Press, (No. 5): 123–138. 46, 49, 51

Kline, R. and Pinch, T. (1996). Users as agents of technological change: The social construction of the automobile in the rural United States. *Technology and Culture*, 37(4): 763–795. DOI: 10.2307/3107097. 30

Kramera, A. D. I., Guillory, J. E., and Hancock, J. T. (2014). Experimental evidence of massive-scale emotional contagion through social networks. *Proceeding of the National Academy of Sciences* 111(24): 8788–8790. DOI: 10.1073/pnas.1320040111.

Latour, B. (1987). *Science in Action: How to Follow Scientists and Engineers Through Society*. Cambridge, MA: Harvard University Press. 3

Latour, B. (1999). *Pandoras Hope, Essays on the Reality of Science Studies*. Cambridge, MA: Harvard University Press. 70

Latour, B. (2004). Why has critique run out of steam? From matters of fact to matters of concern. *Critical Inquiry*, 30(2): 225–248. DOI: 10.1086/421123. 41

Latour, B. (2005). *Reassembling the Social - An Introduction to Actor-Network-Theory*, Oxford: Oxford University Press. 41

Latour, B. and Weibel, P. (Eds.) (2005). *Making Things Public: Atmospheres of Democracy*. Cambridge, MA: MIT Press. 70

Lave, J. and Wenger, E. (1991). *Situated Learning: Legitimate Peripheral Participation*. Cambridge: Cambridge University Press. DOI: 10.1017/CBO9780511815355. xiv

Law, J. (1992). Notes on the theory of the actor-network: Ordering, strategy, and heterogeneity. *Systemic Practice and Action Research*, 5(4): 379–393. DOI: 10.1007/BF01059830. 3

Law, J. (2009). Actor network theory and material semiotics. In *The New Blackwell Companion to Social Theory*, Turner, B. S., Ed. Blackwell: 141–158. 3

Lawson, B. (2004). *What Designers Know*. New York: Routledge. 49, 50

Lawson, B. (2006). *How Designers Think*, 4th ed. New York: Routledge. 49

Lee, R. B. (1979). *The !Kung San: Men, Women and Work in a Foraging Society*. Cambridge and New York: Cambridge University Press. 38

Leidner, R. (1993). *Fast Food. Fast Talk: Service Work and the Routinization of Everyday Life*. Berkeley, CA: University of California Press. 41

Lessig, L. (2005). Commons on the Wires, In *Creative Industries*, Hartley, J., Ed.). Oxford: Blackwell. 59

Lévi-Strauss, C. (1966). *The Savage Mind*. University of Chicago Press. 4

Ljungblad, S. and Holmquist, L. E. (2007). Transfer scenarios: grounding innovation with marginal practices. In *Proceedings of the SIGCHI Conference on Human Factors in Computing Systems*. ACM: 737–746. DOI: 10.1145/1240624.1240738. 75

Lovelock, C. H. (1996). *Services Marketing*, 3rd ed. Upper Saddle River, NJ: Prentice Hall. 11

Lovelock, C., and Gummesson, E. (2004). Whither services marketing? In search of a new paradigm and fresh perspectives. *Journal of Service Research*, 7(1): 20–41. DOI: 10.1177/1094670504266131. 35

Lovelock, C.H. and Wirtz, J. (2004). *Services Marketing: People, Technology, and Strategy*. Englewood Cliffs, NJ: Prentice Hall. 33

Lusch, R. F. and Vargo, S. L. (2006). Service-dominant logic: reactions, reflections and refinements. *Marketing Theory*, 6(3): 281–288. DOI: 10.1177/1470593106066781.

Lynch, M. (2001). Ethnomethodology and the logic of practice. In *The Practice Turn in Contemporary Theory*, Schatzki, T. R., Knorr-Cetina, K., and von Savigny, E., Eds. New York: Routledge: 140–157. 3

Macdonald, C. L. and Sirianni, C. (Eds.) (1996). *Working in the Service Society*. Philadelphis, PA: Temple University Press. 41

MacKenzie, D. and Wajcman, J. (Eds.) (1999). *The Social Shaping of Technology*. 2nd ed. Buckingham, UK: Open University Press. 30

Maffei, S., Mager, B., and Sangiorgi, D. (2005). Innovation through service design. From research and theory to a network of practice. A user's driven perspective. *Joining Forces*. Helsinki, Finland: University of Art and History. 57

Maglio, P. P., Srinivasan, S., Kreulen, J. T., and Spohrer, J. (2006). Service systems, service scientists, SSME, and innovation. *Communications of the ACM*, 49(7): 81–85. DOI: 10.1145/1139922.1139955. 33

Maglio, P.P., Vargo, S.L., Caswell, N., and Spohrer, J. (2009). The service system is the basic abstraction of service science. *Information Systems and e-Business Management*, 7: 395–406. DOI: 10.1007/s10257-008-0105-1. 33, 42

Malinowski, B. (1922). *Argonauts of the Western Pacific*. New York: Dutton. 23

McFadyen, L. (2012). The time it takes to make: Design and use in architecture and anthropology. In *Design and Anthropology*, Gunn, W, and Donovan, J., Eds. (2012). . Burlington VT: Ashgate: 101–119. 50

Meroni, A. and Sangiorgi, D. (2011). A new discipline. In *Design for Services*. Gower Publishing. 41, 59, 61, 63, 68

Merton, R. K. (1968). *Social Theory and Social Structure*. New York: The Free Press. 68

Miaskiewicz, T. and Kozar, K. A. (2011). Personas and user-centered design: how can personas benefit product design processes? *Design Studies*, 32(5): 417–430. DOI: 10.1016/j.destud.2011.03.003. 63

Miettinen, S. and Koivisto, M. (Eds.) (2009). *Designing Services with Innovative Methods*. Helsinki: University of Art and Design. ISBN: 978-952-5018-42-4. 66

Morelli, N. (2002). Designing product/service systems: A methodological exploration1. *Design Issues*, 18(3): 3–17. DOI: 10.1162/074793602320223253. 64, 65

Morelli, N. and Tollestrup, C. (2009). New representation techniques for designing in a systemic perspective. *Nordes*, (2). 63

Mosse, D. (2005). *Cultivating Development: An Ethnography of Aid Policy and Practice*. Ann Arbor, MI: Pluto Press. 56

Nelson, H. G., and Stolterman, E. (2003). *The Design Way: Intentional Change in an Unpredictable World: Foundations and Fundamentals of Design Competence*. Englewood Cliffs, NJ: Educational Technology Publications. 47

Oakes, G. (1990). *The Soul of the Salesman: The Moral Ethos of Personal Sales*. Atlantic Highlands, NJ: Humanities Press International. 41

OECD, (2005). *Growth in Services: Fostering Employment, Productivity and Innovation*, Meeting of the OECD Council at Ministerial Level. 13

Oliver, R. L., Rust, R. T., and Varki, S. (1997). Customer delight: foundations, findings, and managerial insight. *Journal of Retailing*, 73(3): 311–336. DOI: 10.1016/S0022-4359(97)90021-X. 33

Ortner, S. B. (1984). Theory in anthropology since the sixties. *Contemporary Studies in Society and History* 26(1): 126–166. DOI: 10.1017/S0010417500010811. 2

Ortner, S. B. (2006). Anthropology and social theory. In *Culture, Power and the Acting Subject*, S.B. Ortner. Durham, NC and London: Duke University Press. DOI: 10.1215/9780822388456. 2

Ostrom, A. L., Bitner, M. J., Brown, S. W., Burkhard, K. A., Goul, M., Smith-Daniels, V., Demirkan, H., and Rabinovich, E. (2010). Moving forward and making a difference: research priorities for the science of service. *Journal of Service Research*, (13): 4–36. DOI: 10.1177/1094670509357611. 55

Patrício, L., Fisk, R.P., and e Cunha, J.F. (2008). Designing multi-interface service experiences: The service experience blueprint, *Journal of Service Research*, 10(4): 318–334. DOI: 10.1177/1094670508314264. 60

Pinch, T. J. and Bijker, W. E. (1984). The social construction of facts and artefacts: Or how the sociology of science and the sociology of technology might benefit each other. *Social Studies of Science*, 14(3): 399–441. DOI: 10.1177/030631284014003004. 30

Pine, J. B. and Gilmore, J.H. (1998). Welcome to the experience economy. *Harvard Business Review*, 76 (July 4–August), 97–105. 40

Pine, J. B. and Gilmore, J.H. (1999). *The Experience Economy: Work Is Theatre and Every Business a Stage*. Boston: Harvard Business School Press. 40, 45

Plattner, S. (Ed.). (1989). *Economic Anthropology*. Stanford, CA: Stanford University Press. 11

Polaine, A., Lovlie, L., and Reason, B. (2013). *Service Design: From Insight to Implementaion*. Brooklyn, NY: Rosenfeld Media. 55

Prahalad, C. K. and Ramaswamy, V. (2004). *The Future of Competition: Co-Creating Unique Value with Customers*. Boston: Harvard Business School Press. 57

Radcliffe-Brown, A. R. (1952). *Structure and Function in Primitive Society*. Glencoe, IL: The Free Press. 43

Reckwitz, A. (2002). Toward a theory of social practices: A development in culturalist theorizing. *European Journal of Social Theoery*, 5(2): 243–263. DOI: 10.1177/13684310222225432. 2, 3

Redström, J. (2006). Towards user design? On the shift from object to user as the subject of design. *Design Studies*, 27(2): 123–139. DOI: 10.1016/j.destud.2005.06.001. 69

Redström, J. (2008). RE: Definitions of use. *Design Studies*, 29: 410–423. DOI: 10.1016/j.destud.2008.05.001. 69

Rosson, M. B. and Carroll, J. M. (2012). Scenario based design. In *The Human Computer Interaction Handbook*. Jacko, J. Ed. Boca Raton, FL: CRC Press: 1105–1124.

Rothman, R. (1998). *Working: Sociological Perspective*, London: Prentice Hall. 19

Rowe, P. G. (1998). *Design Thinking*. Cambridge MA: MIT Press. 46, 49

Rushton, A. M. and Carson, D. J. (1989). The marketing of services: managing the intangibles. *European Journal of Marketing*, 23(8): 23–44. DOI: 10.1108/EUM0000000000582. 35

Saco, R. and Gonsalves, A. (2008), Service design: An appraisal. *Design Management Journal*, 19(1): 10–19. DOI: 10.1111/j.1948-7169.2008.tb00101.x. 34, 55, 56, 57, 59

Saha, S., Beach, M. C., and Cooper, L. A. (2008). Patient centeredness, cultural competence and healthcare quality. *Journal National Medical Association*, 100(11): 1275–1285. 40

Sangiorgi, D., Prendiville, A., and Rickettes, A. (Eds.) (2014). *Mapping and Developing Service Design Research in the UK*. SDR: Service Design Research Network. (available at www.servicedesignresearch.com/uk/). 59

Sangiorgi, D., Hands, D., and Murphy, E. (2014). *Proceedings of the Fourth Service Design and Service Innovation Conference*. Lancaster University, U.K.: April 9–11, 2014. xiii

Schatzki, T. R. (1996). *Social Practices. A Wittgensteinian Approach to Human Activity and the Social*. Cambridge: Cambridge University Press. DOI: 10.1017/CBO9780511527470. 2

Schatzki, T. R. (2001). Introduction: practice theory. In *The Practice Turn in Contemporary Theory*, Schatzki, T. R., Knorr-Cetina, K., and von Savigny, E., Eds. Londom. UK: Routledge: 10–23. 2, 74

Schatzki, T. R. (2002). *The Site of the Social. A Philosophical Account of the Constitution of Social Life and Change.* University Park, PA: The Pennsylvania State University Press. 2

Schiffer, M. B. (2010). *Behavioral Archaeology: Principles and Practice.* Oakville CT: Equinox. 51

Schuler, D. and Namioka, A. (Eds.), (1993). *Participatory Design. Principles and Practices.* Hillsdale NJ: Lawrence Erlbaum Associates. 58

Secomandi, F. and Snelders, D. (2011). The object of service design. *Design Issues*, 27(3), 20–34. DOI: 10.1162/DESI_a_00088. 60

Segal, D. A. and Yanagisako, S. A. (Eds.) (2005). *Unwrapping the Sacred Bundle: Reflections on the Disciplining of Anthropology*, Durham, NC: Duke University Press. DOI: 10.1215/9780822386841. 43

Seyfang, G. (2004). Time banks: rewarding community self-help in the inner city? *Community Development Journal*, 39(1), 62–71. DOI: 10.1093/cdj/39.1.62. 17

Seyfang, G. (2006). Harnessing the potential of the social economy? Time banks and UK public policy. *International Journal of Sociology and Social Policy*, 26(9/10), 430–443. DOI: 10.1108/01443330610690569. 17

Shaw, C. and Ivens, J. (2002). *Building Great Customer Experiences.* New York, Palgrave MacMillan. DOI: 10.1057/9780230554719.

Shostack, G. L. (1982). How to design a service. *European Journal of Marketing*, 16(1), 49–63. DOI: 10.1108/EUM0000000004799. 63

Shostack, G. L. (1984). Designing services that deliver. *Harvard Business Review*, 62(1), 133–139. 64, 65

Shostack, G. L. (1985). Planning the service encounter. In *The Service Encounter*, Czepiel, J. A., Solomon, M. R., and Surprenant, C. F., Eds. Lexington, MA: Lexington Books: 243–254. 39

Simon, H. A. (1981). *The Sciences of the Artificial.* 1969. Massachusetts Institute of Technology. 46

Simonsen, J. and Roberson, T. (Eds.) (2012). *Routledge International Handbook of Participatory Design.* London, Routledge. 58

Singleton, B. (2009). Services design in new territories. *IASDR, Rigor and Relevance in Design.* 58

Smart Cities. Guide to using customer journey mapping. Smart Cities Brief number 12. Accessed on January 29, 2015 at http://www.slideshare.net/smartcities/smart-cities-a-guide-to-using-customer-journey-mapping. 67

Spohrer, J. and Maglio, P. P. (2008). The emergence of service science: Towards systematic service innovations to accelerate the coproduction of value. *Production and Operations Management*, (17)3: 238–246. DOI: 10.3401/poms.1080.0027. 33, 42

Spohrer, J. and Maglio, P. (2010). Toward a science of service systems. In *Handbook of Service Science*. In Maglio, P. P., Kieliszewski, C. A., and Spohrer, J. C., Eds. New York: Springer: 157–194. DOI: 10.1007/978-1-4419-1628-0_9. 33, 42

Star, S. L. (1991a). The sociology of the invisible: The primacy of work in the writings of Anselm Strauss. In *Social Organization and Social Process: Essays in Honor of Anselm Strauss*, Maines, D., Ed. Hawthorne, NY: Aldine de Gruyter: 265–283. 60

Star, S. L. (1991b). Invisible work and silenced dialogues in knowledge representation. In *Women, Work and Computerization: Understanding and Overcoming Bias in Work and Education*, Eriksson, I. V., Kitchenham, B. A., and Tijdens, K. G., Eds. Helsinki, Finland, June 30–July 2 1991. Amsterdam: Elsevier Science Publishers B.V. (North-Holland): 81–92. 60

Steinberg, R. J. and Figart, D. M. (1999). Emotional labor since the managed heart. *The Annals of the American Academy of Political and Social Science*, 561(1): 8–26. DOI: 10.1177/0002716299561001001. 41

Stickdorn, M. and Schneider, J. (2010). *This is Service Design Thinking*. Amsterdam: BIS Publishers. 55, 66

Stolterman, E. (2008). The nature of design practice and implications for interaction design research. *International Journal of Design*, 2(1), 55–65. 45

Suchman, L. (2000). Organizing alignment: A case of bridge-building. *Organization*, 7(2), 311–327. DOI: 10.1177/135050840072007. 4, 6

Suchman, L. (2002). Located accountabilities in technology production. *Scandinavian Journal of Information Systems*, 14(2):91–105. 58

Suchman, L.A. (2007). *Human–Machine Reconfigurations: Plans and Situated Actions*. Cambridge: Cambridge University Press. 38

Suchman, L., Blomberg, J., Orr, J. E., and Trigg, R. (1999). Reconstructing technologies as social practice. *American Behavioral Scientist*, 43(3), 392–408. DOI: 10.1177/00027649921955335.

Suchman, L., Trigg, R., and Blomberg, J. (2002). Working artefacts: Ethnomethods of the prototype. *The British Journal of Sociology*, 53(2), 163–179. DOI: 10.1080/00071310220133287.

Teboul, J. (2006). *Service is Front Stage: Positioning Services for Value Advantage.* New York: Palgrave MacMillian. DOI: 10.1057/9780230579477. 12, 33, 35

Thackara, J. (2005). *In the Bubble: Designing in a Complex World.* Cambridge: MIT. 16, 17, 45, 56, 58, 61

Thomke, S. (2003). R&D comes to services: Bank of America's pathbreaking experiments. *Harvard Business Review,* April. 68

Thrift, N. (2006). Re-inventing invention: new tendencies in capitalist commodification. *Economy and Society Volume,* 35(2): 279–306. DOI: 10.1080/03085140600635755. 59

Trigg, R. H., Blomberg, J., and Suchman, L. (1999). Moving document collections online: The evolution of a shared repository. In *ECSCW'99.* Netherlands: Springer, 331–350. DOI: 10.1007/978-94-011-4441-4_18.

Vargo, S. L. and Lusch, R. F. (2004a). The four service marketing myths: Remnants of a goods-based, manufacturing model. *Journal of Service Research,* 6(4), 324–335. DOI: 10.1177/1094670503262946. 35

Vargo, S. L. and Lusch, R. F. (2004b). Evolving to a new dominant logic for marketing. *Journal of Marketing,* 68: 1–17. DOI: 10.1509/jmkg.68.1.1.24036. 37

Vargo, S. L. and Lusch, R. F. (2006). Service-dominant logic: What it is, what it is not, what it might be. In *The Service-Dominant Logic of Marketing: Dialog, Debate and Directions,* Lusch, R. F. and Vargo, S. L., Eds. Armonk, NY: M.E. Sharpe, Inc.: 43–56. 35

Vargo, S. L. and Lusch, R. F. (2008a). Service-dominant logic: Continuing the evolution. *Journal of the Academy of Marketing Science,* 36: 1–10. DOI: 10.1007/s11747-007-0069-6. 36, 37

Vargo, S. L. and Lusch, R. F. (2008b). "Why service?," *Journal of the Academy of Marketing Science,* 36: 25–38. DOI: 10.1007/s11747-007-0068-7. 35

Vargo, S. L. and Lusch, R. F. (2011). It's all B2B...and beyond: Toward a systems perspective of the market. *Industrial Marketing Management,* 40: 181–187. DOI: 10.1016/j.indmarman.2010.06.026. 33, 36

Vargo, S. T., Maglio, P. P., and Akaka, M. A. (2008). On value and value co-creation: A service systems and service logic perspective, *European Management Journal,* (26)3: 145–152. DOI: 10.1016/j.emj.2008.04.003. 33, 42

Vezzoli, C. and Manzini, E. (2008). *Design for Environmental Sustainability.* London: Springer. 58

Von Hippel, E. (2009). Democratizing innovation: the evolving phenomenon of user innovation. *International Journal of Innovation Science,* 1(1), 29–40. DOI: 10.1260/175722209787951224. 59

Voss, A., Hartswood, M., Procter, R., Rouncefield, M., Slack, R., and Büscher, M. (Eds.) (2009). *Configuring User-Designer Relations: Interdisciplinary Perspectives*. London: Springer. 69

Wahl, D. C. and Baxter, S. (2008). The designer's role in facilitating sustainable solutions. *Design Issues*, 24(2), 72–83. DOI: 10.1162/desi.2008.24.2.72. 47

Watson, J. L. (1997). *Golden Arches East: McDonald's in East Asia*. Stanford, CA: Stanford University Press. 30

Winograd, T. (1997). From computing machinery to interaction design. In *Beyond Calculation: The Next Fifty Years of Computing*, Denning, P. and Metcalfe, R., Eds. New York: Springer-Verlag: 149–162. 45

World Bank Group (2000). Chapter IX—Growth of the Service Sector. In *Beyond Economic Growth: Meeting the Challenges of Economic Development*. The International Bank for Reconstruction and Development: The World Bank. 14

Zeisel, J. (2006). *Inquiry by Design: Environment/Behavior/Neuroscience in Architecture, Interiors, Landscape, and Planning*. New York: WW Norton and Co. 48, 49

Zeithaml, V. A. (1981). How consumer evaluation processes differ between goods and services. Marketing of Services, 9(1), 25–32. 35

Zeithaml, V. A., Parasuraman, A., and Berry, L. L. (1985). Problems and strategies in services marketing. *Journal of Marketing*, 49 (Spring): 33–46. DOI: 10.2307/1251563. 35, 36

Zeithaml, V. A. and Bitner, M. J. (1996). *Services Marketing*. New York: The McGraw-Hill Companies, Inc. 11

Zeithaml, V. A., Bitner, M. J., and Gremler, D. D. (2006). *Services Marketing: Integrating Customer Focus Across the Firm* (4th ed.). Boston: McGraw-Hill/Irwin. 66

Zeithaml, V. A., Bitner, M. J. and Gremler, D. D. (2009). *Services Marketing: Integrating Customer Focus Across the Firm*, 5th ed., New York: McGraw-Hill.

Zimmerman, J., Forlizzi, J., and Evenson, S. (2007). Research through design as a method for interaction design research in HCI. In *Proceedings of the SIGCHI conference on Human Factors in Computing Systems*. ACM: 493–502. DOI: 10.1145/1240624.1240704. 45

Zomerdijk, L.G., and Voss C.A., (2010). Service design for experience-centric services. *Journal of Service Research*, 13(1): 67–82. DOI: 10.1177/1094670509351960. 60, 63

Author Biographies

Jeanette Blomberg is an anthropologist who has worked in high tech, corporate research contexts for over three decades—first at the Xerox Palo Alto Research Center (PARC), later at Sapient Corporation, and currently at IBM Research. Along the way she has been an industry-affiliated professor at the Blekinge Institute of Technology in Sweden where she received an honorary doctorate in 2011. Her research includes a critical assessment of the promise of data analytics within the context of the enterprise, designing ethnographically informed organizational interventions, and participatory design.

Chuck Darrah is professor and chair of the Department of Anthropology at San Jose State University. His research focuses on work, workplaces, families, and technology. He co-founded the Silicon Valley Cultures Project and later the Human Aspiration and Design Laboratory (HADLab), both at San Jose State University.

Printed in the United States
by Baker & Taylor Publisher Services